THE INV

MANAGING YOUR INVESTMENTS, SAVINGS AND CREDIT

THE BASICS AND BEYOND

ESMÉ E. FAERBER

PROBUS PUBLISHING COMPANY
Chicago, Illinois

© 1992, Esmé Faerber

ALL RIGHTS RESERVED. No part of this publication may be reproduced, stored in a retrieval system, or transmitted by any means, electronic, mechanical, photocopying recording, or otherwise, without the prior written permission of the publisher and the copyright holder.

This publication is designed to provide accurate and authoritative information in regard to the subject matter covered. It is sold with the understanding that neither the author nor the publisher are engaged in rendering legal, accounting or other professional service. If legal or other expert assistance is required, the services of a competent professional should be sought

ISBN 1-55738-245-X

Printed in the United States of America

IPC

1   2   3   4   5   6   7   8   9   0

CONTENTS

Preface   v

Chapter 1: Personal Financial Statements   1
     1.1   Balance Sheet   1
     1.2   Analysis of the Balance Sheet   6
     1.3   Income Statement   7
     1.4   Analysis of the Income Statement   10
     1.5   Formulating a Budget   11
     1.6   Analysis of the Budget   15

Chapter 2: Personal and Financial Record Keeping   21
     2.1   What Records To Keep and Where To Keep Them   21
     2.2   What Tax Records To Keep and How To Prepare
          for Your Accountant   28
     2.3   How Long To Keep Records   31
     2.4   How To Reconcile Your Checking Account   34

Chapter 3: How To Save Money   41
     3.1   Savings Objectives   41
     3.2   Investor Guidelines   48

Chapter 4: How To Read the Financial Pages   53
     4.1   What Is the State of the Economy?   53
     4.2   The Effects of the Economy on the Stock Markets   55
     4.3   Monetary Policy and the Financial Markets   56
     4.4   Fiscal Policy and the Markets   60
     4.5   The Stock Markets and How To Read Stock Prices   61
     4.6   The Bond Markets and How To Read Bond Prices   68
     4.7   How To Read Mutual Funds Quotations   74

Chapter 5: How Well Are My Investments Doing?   77
     5.1   What Is My Rate of Return?   77
     5.2   The Greatest Return May Not Be the Best   80
     5.3   How To Measure Rates of Return   82

iv   Contents

5.4	How Can You Improve Your Rates of Return?	85
5.5	Caveats for Investors	89

Chapter 6: Overview of Credit   91

6.1	Reasons for Consumer Borrowing	91
6.2	The Types of Credit and Their Costs	93
6.3	What to Do if You Are Denied Credit	113
6.4	What Are the Alternatives if You Cannot Pay Your Debts?	115

Chapter 7: Automobile and Housing Decisions   119

7.1	New or Used Automobile?	119
7.2	What Type of Car?	122
7.3	How To Purchase a Car	122
7.4	Renting Decisions	127
7.5	Home Ownership	129
7.6	Should You Rent or Buy?	132
7.7	Guidelines for Buying a Home	133
7.8	Second Homes	135
7.9	Time-Sharing	137

Appendix   139

1	Safe Haven Savings Instruments	139
2	Bonds	143
3	Closed-End Funds	163
4	Common Stock	166
5	Convertible Securities	169
6	Mutual Funds (Open-Ended Funds)	173
7	Preferred Stock	179
8	Treasury Bills	183
9	U.S. Savings Bonds	186

References   191

About the Author   193

PREFACE

Managing Your Investments, Savings and Credit: The Basics and Beyond
is designed to meet the specific needs of those who require a basic guide
to personal finance.

This book explains in detail:

- The steps in compiling financial statements and their uses.

- The management of personal finance.

- Savings and investment criteria and a detailed discussion of
  the most common investment instruments.

- What everyone should know about credit and its uses particularly with major purchases, namely automobiles and homes.

The preparation of this manuscript has been greatly facilitated by
the people at Probus Publishing Company. A special note of thanks to
my husband, Eric, for his thoughtful criticism while proofreading the
manuscript at different stages of its development, and to our children,
Jennifer and Michael, for their continued support.

Esmé Faerber
October 1991

CHAPTER 1

Personal Financial Statements

Are you the type of person who feels that anything concerning financial matters should automatically be referred to an accountant? You don't need to be a CPA (Certified Public Accountant) or have an MBA (Master of Business Administration degree) in order to manage your finances. The principles for constructing personal financial statements are the same as those used for corporate financial statements, except that the former are much simpler to do (and well worth the effort). Financial statements are the starting point in your financial planning.

Without information provided by financial statements, you will not know what you are worth or whether you can afford to buy something now or in the future. There are many occasions when knowingly or unknowingly, you have constructed your personal financial statements — when filling out the many application forms needed for home mortgages or when applying for credit cards. After all, why would a bank lend money if it could not assess the financial risks by studying a financial profile of the borrower?

The most important financial statements are the *balance sheet* — a statement which summarizes your financial wealth at one point in time — and the *income statement* which shows what has happened to your financial condition over a period of time.

1.1 Balance Sheet

Your personal balance sheet shows wealth at a particular date in time. It is a still photograph of your financial situation.

The three major components of a balance sheet are:

Assets: things of value that are owned;
Liabilities: amounts of money that are owed;
Net Worth: the difference between assets and liabilities.

The accounting equation in the balance sheet can be stated as follows:

Figure 1.1

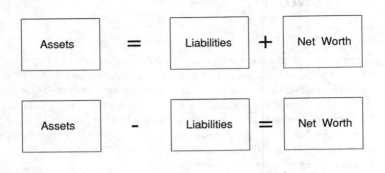

Assets

Assets are the items of value that you own which include items not fully paid for. For example, if you bought a car for $10,000 and paid $1,000 in cash, financing the balance, you would record the car as an asset worth $10,000 and the auto loan as a liability of $9,000.

Assets may be broken down into two types—financial and nonfinancial.

Financial Assets provide income or a rate of return. These would include:

- cash
- savings accounts
- mutual funds
- bonds
- cash surrender values of life insurance policies
- limited partnerships
- checking accounts
- money market funds
- stocks
- ownership in businesses
- investment pools

Nonfinancial Assets are those owned for the pleasure and benefits that they give, although they can also provide income. These would include:

- homes
- boats
- jewelry
- art
- clothing
- automobiles
- furniture
- antiques
- coin/stamp collections

The distinction between the two asset classifications may be blurred for certain assets. For example, a rental property would be classified as a financial asset due to its earning capacity. Yet, a non interest-bearing checking account is a financial asset despite the fact that it does not provide a return.

The first step in compiling a balance sheet is to list all assets at their fair market value if available. Bear in mind that the emphasis is on the current fair market value. An automobile that was purchased six months ago will have a significant decline in value (depending on the type of car, the loss in value could be as much as 10 to 20 percent in the first year). Not all assets lose their value over time. Some may appreciate. They include: real estate, jewelry, collectibles such as art, antiques, stamps and coins.

Table 1.1 shows the hypothetical balance sheet of a couple we will call Mr. & Mrs. X. The first item in the financial asset category is *cash* followed by *cash equivalents*. The latter would include money market mutual funds and savings accounts.

Stocks and *bonds* are listed at their market value. The current prices of stocks and bonds which are listed on the exchanges can be found in the financial sections of the daily newspapers. Market values for unlisted stocks and bonds can be obtained from a stockbroker. Listed stocks and bonds can be easily converted into cash due to their marketability, but you may be reluctant to convert them if their market prices are lower or higher than their purchase price.

The major asset in the nonfinancial section for most families is *real estate*. This includes your homes — personal residence, vacation home and/or condominiums. (Investment property would be included in the financial section.) Real estate should be listed at its estimated fair market value — have it appraised by a real estate broker or track selling prices for similar houses in your neighborhood.

The market value for personal *household assets* is difficult to assess. Such assets should be valued conservatively, because a forced sale to raise cash often brings less than market value. For example, a five-year-old stereo system would be worth much less than its original purchase price.

When Mr. & Mrs. X's assets have been totaled, their worth is $238,300. This leads to the next question — who provided the financing for these assets? If they are financed by institutions or others, they are liabilities, but if Mr. & Mrs. X financed them, they are part of Mr. & Mrs. X's net worth.

4   Chapter 1

Table 1.1

Mr. & Mrs. X
Personal Balance Sheet
as of December 31, 1991

ASSETS		LIABILITIES	
FINANCIAL		CURRENT	
Checking Accounts	$ 700	Credit Card Balances	$ 2,160
Savings Accounts	5,000	Department Store Charges	900
Money Market Funds	7,000	**Total Current Liabilities**	**3,060**
Equity Mutual Funds	15,000		
Stocks	15,000	LONG-TERM LIABILITIES	
Municipal Bonds	10,500	Auto Loan	8,000
Cash Surrender Value		Mortgages:	
of Life Insurance	5,000	Home	30,000
Keoghs, IRAs	6,000	Condominium	25,400
Total Financial Assets	**64,200**	Long-Term Liabilities	63,400
NONFINANCIAL ASSETS		TOTAL LIABILITES	66,460
Home	90,000		
Condominium	60,000		
Automobiles	12,000		
Computer, Stereo, TVs	2,500		
Furniture	4,500		
Clothing	2,000		
Jewelry	3,100		
Total Nonfinancial Assets	**174,100**	**Net Worth**	**171,840**
		TOTAL LIABILITIES AND	
TOTAL ASSETS	**238,300**	**NET WORTH**	**238,300**

Liabilities

Liabilities are the amounts of money owed to others and can be broken down into two categories:

Current Liabilities are debts that must be paid within a short period of time. They include credit card charges, utility bills, rent (if you don't own a home), medical and dental bills.

Long-Term debt should be listed at its current outstanding balance and not at the amount of the original loan. For example, in Mr. and Mrs. X's balance sheet, their home mortgage was originally $40,000 but with part of their monthly payments applied to reducing their balance owed, their outstanding balance as of the balance sheet date is $30,000. Interest is charged on all loans and is the other component in the monthly payment (the monthly payment consists of interest and the principal reduction) which is not included as part of the current outstanding loan balance. Mortgage lenders, banks and financial institutions will always provide their clients, on request, with the current outstanding balance as of the beginning or end of the month.

Mr. and Mrs. X have total liabilities of $66,460 — less than their total assets. When assets are less than liabilities, a person is technically insolvent and will more than likely have difficulty making scheduled payments. This situation could lead to bankruptcy.

Net Worth

Net worth is the difference between total assets and total liabilities. Mr. and Mrs. X's net worth is $171,840 ($238,300 less $66,460). Assuming that they could sell all of their assets at the values listed on the balance sheet and pay off all their liabilities, the Xs would have $171,840 left. Since selling off all assets is an unlikely scenario, net worth should not be thought of as cash to spend. Rather, net worth is a measure of a person's financial position as of the date of the balance sheet.

Net worth can be increased by:

- an increase in salary, wages and/or profits;

- a reduction in living expenses;

- acquiring assets;

- reducing liabilities.

6   Chapter 1

1.2   Analysis of the Balance Sheet

The importance of increasing net worth is obvious but the addition of assets does not always increase your net worth. It depends on whether these assets are acquired through ownership or through financing. For example, if you borrow $80,000 to buy a Porsche for $80,000, your net worth remains unchanged. You would actually have less of an ownership stake than someone who buys a Hyundai for $7,000 in cash. Besides the ownership stake, you will lose more in depreciation on your Porsche than the Hyundai owner will lose in the first year. Net worth can be increased by adding assets through ownership rather than spending the money frivolously.

Net worth will also increase through appreciation of assets. Consider the houses that were bought fifteen years ago for $70,000 and are currently worth $500,000 — or stock portfolios that have doubled in value.

The flip side of the coin involves paying off liabilities. This will increase net worth if assets remain the same.

Net worth can decline for many reasons — including the overuse of debt and depreciating assets. The $80,000 Porsche may depreciate more in the first year so that the car is worth less than the amount of the loan.

By compiling a personal balance sheet every year, you can compare whether your net worth is increasing, decreasing or remaining the same. You can also analyze the asset structure and compare how assets have grown/declined or stayed the same. For example, in Mr. and Mrs. X's case, their nonfinancial assets are almost three times the amount of their financial assets ($174,100 as opposed to $64,200). Looked at another way, nonfinancial assets are 73.1 percent ($174,100/238,300) of total assets and financial assets are 26.9 percent ($64,200/238,300) of total assets.

The X's largest assets are real estate (the home and condominium), accounting for 86.2 percent ($150,000/174,100) of the nonfinancial assets and 62.9 percent ($150,000/238,300) of the total assets. This is not uncommon for most young families; as they approach the years when their earnings peak, they will be able to build up their financial assets.

Mr. and Mrs. X have $66,460 in liabilities, $3,060 of which is current. Generally, short-term debts are repaid out of current monthly income but if Mr. and Mrs. X suddenly lost their present jobs, they would have to sell off some of their assets to repay the $3,060. They would use their most liquid financial assets (those that can be easily converted to cash without losing any of the principal in the conversion). Mr. and Mrs. X have good coverage – $12,700 of liquid assets to $3,060 of current liabilities. Consequently, the relationship between liquid financial assets and current liabilities and the relationship between total assets and total liabilities should be checked from year to year to see whether there is an over extension of debt.

When your yearly balance sheet shows that your net worth is increasing, your financial wealth is growing.

1.3 Income Statement

The *income statement* shows income and expenditures over a period of time, whereas the balance sheet shows financial position at a single point in time.

The income statement is comprised of three major parts:

- income received during the time period;
- expenditures made during the time period;
- surplus/deficit of income over expenditures.

Income

The main source of income for most of us is the money we earn from our occupations in the form of wages, salaries, commissions and self-employment income. Other sources of income include bonuses, interest, dividends, gains on the sale of assets, rent, income from pensions, payments for alimony and child support, social security income, gifts and inheritances. All sources of income should be included in order to make the income statement complete.

Table 1.2 shows the income statement for the year ended 1991 for Mr. and Mrs. X. Mr. X has an annual salary of $50,000 but after deductions and payroll taxes (federal, state and social security), his take home pay is $3,000 per month or $36,000 for the year. Payroll taxes and deductions are shown as expenditures.

Mrs. X has her own business which recorded a net profit (all revenues minus all expenses) of $30,000 for the 1991 year. If actual

8   Chapter 1

Table 1.2

INCOME STATEMENT FOR MR. AND MRS. X
FOR THE YEAR ENDED DECEMBER 31, 1991

INCOME

Mr. X's Salary	$50,000	
Mrs. X's Employment Income-Profits	30,000	
Interest and Dividends	3,450	
Gain on Sale of Stocks	1,220	
Tax Refund	2,500	
TOTAL INCOME		$87,170

EXPENDITURES

Food	6,200	
Clothing	2,260	
Mortgages	8,860	
Telephone & Utilities	2,050	
Insurance-Homes	550	
Insurance-Life & Disability	3,600	
Medical & Dental Expenses	960	
Child Care Payments	6,000	
Automobile Loan Payments	3,600	
Automobile Expenses & Insurance	2,500	
Real Estate Taxes	2,450	
Social Security Taxes	3,825	
Federal, State & Local Taxes	13,305	
IRA & Keogh Contributions	4,900	
Charitable Contributions	2,000	
Recreation	2,000	
Summer Vacation	2,500	
TOTAL EXPENDITURES		67,560

SURPLUS $19,610

---

figures for the coming year are not available, they can be estimated. It may also be necessary to estimate the amount of dividends, based on the past payout ratios of those stocks, if an income statement is projected for the future year. When in doubt, income should be underestimated rather than overestimated.

Mr. and Mrs. X bought and sold common stocks during the year which resulted in net capital gains of $1,220. Gains from the sale of any other assets should be included as income.

Expenditures

The second major category in the income statement is *expenditures* which shows where money was spent. The types of expenditures to include in the income statement will depend on the complexity of your financial matters. Major categories of expenditure should be listed but there is no need to account for every penny spent. Categories of expenditures can be developed by reviewing checkbook records, credit card statements and the more difficult task of tracing any cash payments. By adding the payments made in each category, you will have a fairly accurate account of your expenditures for the year.

Most of Mr. and Mrs. X's expenditures are for living and shelter. This is true for most families but particularly-young families whose incomes have not reached their full potential.

Mr. and Mrs. X have some *fixed expenses* which do not vary from month to month such as mortgage payments, auto installment loan payments, insurance premiums and child care payments.

Variable expenses are those that change from month to month such as food, clothing, telephone, utilities, medical and dental expenses, gas and auto repairs, household operating expenses and repairs, contributions and recreational expenses.

Surplus or Deficit

When income exceeds expenditures, there is a *surplus*; a *deficit* is recorded when spending exceeds the amount of income for the period. A deficit on the personal level is no different from that on a national level — the U.S. government deficit, for example. There is a major exception between the two — the U.S. government has available sources to finance growing deficit spending year after year, which is not available on the personal level. The government can print money and increase the

Figure 1.2   Deficit, etc.

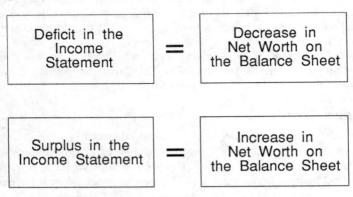

amount of debt that it auctions on a weekly and/or monthly basis to finance deficit spending.

On a personal level, you may draw from savings or use debt to finance deficit spending, which will mean a decrease in net worth. The factor limiting how long this can work is the amount of net worth. The relationship between the income statement and the balance sheet is shown in Figure 1.2.

A surplus represents anything that increases net worth — an additional amount which can be saved, used to acquire assets, or to pay off liabilities. Thus, with all due respect, the U.S. government is not the best role model for increasing financial position.

Mr. and Mrs. X have a surplus of $19,610 for the year 1991, which they then used to buy stocks and bonds. This has increased their net worth from the previous year to $171,840 as of December 31, 1991 (Table 1.1).

1.4   Analysis of the Income Statement

The income statement shows whether you have been successful in living within the limits of your family income. If the amount saved is negligible or there is a deficit, you should check your income and expenditures.

Income is difficult to increase in the short-term, although it can be done, perhaps by finding an additional part-time job. Longer term, income can be increased by establishing yourself in your profession, looking for a better paying job or changing careers. The latter alternative should be deliberated carefully before making any moves.

Expenditures are also difficult to reduce but variable expenditures may be easier to cut than fixed expenditures. For example, it may be easier to reduce recreation, summer vacation and/or entertainment expenses than the necessary living expenses such as food, mortgages, utilities and auto expenses.

By going through the process of compiling an income statement, you can see where money has been spent and where to reduce expenditures if necessary.

Mr. and Mrs. X have a surplus of $19,610 which may or may not be satisfactory depending on their goals or expectations for the year. For example, if they had wanted to save $24,000 for the year to be used to buy a new car, they would have fallen short of their goal.

The income statement is not only an important tool in helping to understand current spending patterns, it also assists with future budgeting.

1.5   Formulating a Budget

Having compiled their financial statements, Mr. and Mrs. X need to determine whether:

- they are living within their income limits;

- their current spending patterns are satisfactory;

- they are saving and investing sufficient amounts to satisfy their financial goals;

- any changes that could be made to satisfy financial goals.

A *budget* is a plan for how you intend to spend your money during the coming month, months, or year. It is an integration based on details of your income statement and balance sheet for the past month, months, or year and a reflection of your financial goals. It expresses what you would like to achieve in terms of spending and savings in the future.

Financial Goals

Financial goals vary from person to person over time. They are important because they determine the purpose of savings and investments. Some common financial goals are:

12   Chapter 1

- buying a new car
- paying off a car loan
- accumulating a specific amount of money
- increasing savings and investments
- taking annual vacations
- buying a house
- buying a larger house
- buying a vacation house
- saving to fund children's education
- providing retirement income.

Some of these are short-term while others are longer term goals. It is often much easier to concentrate on the short-term and neglect long-term goals. However, by assigning priorities to each of the goals and quantifying their cost, you can determine the amount of savings needed to fund them. Table 1.3 contains an example of Mr. and Mrs. X's goals and the amounts needed to achieve them.

Table 1.3   Mr. and Mrs. X's Financial Goals

Goals	(1) Estimated Cost	(2) Priorities	(3) Time Needed	(4) Monthly Amount	(5) Monthly Amount with Time Value of Money
Buy a new car	$24,000	1	12 months	$2,000.00	$1,927.00
Children's college fund	50,000	2	192 months	260.42	129.13
Retirement fund	300,000	3	360 months	833.33	201.29
Replace living room furniture	3,600	4	24 months	150.00	138.82
				3,243.75	$2,396.24

The first column shows the estimated amount of money needed for each goal followed by its priorities. Replacing living room furniture is the lowest of Mr. and Mrs. X's priorities. Column 3 shows when the expenditures will be needed. They hope to buy a car in twelve months time; be able to fund their children's education in sixteen years (192 months); retire in thirty years (360 months); and replace living room furniture in two years.

Column 4 shows the monthly amount needed to finance each goal, calculated as follows:

$$\text{Monthly Amount} = \frac{\text{Estimated Cost}}{\text{Time Needed}}$$

In order to provide the funds to buy a new car for $24,000 in a year's time, Mr. and Mrs. X will need to save $2,000 a month for the next year. If they were to fund all of their goals, they would need total savings of $3,243.75 per month.

The astute reader is apt to disagree on that amount and argue that the Xs will need to save less per month due to the fact that the monthly amounts will be invested which will earn a return. That is correct and so, assuming an 8 percent return on all monthly amounts invested, Mr. and Mrs. X would need total savings of $2,396.24 per month to fund all four goals (Column 5).

Realistically, however, Mr. and Mrs. X would have to save more than the amount in Column 5 to fund all of their goals because of two factors: income taxes and inflation. Income, interest and dividends are all taxed by the federal, state and in some cases local governments, where the average combined tax rate could amount to more than 30 percent of adjusted gross income.

Inflation pushes up prices, thereby eroding future purchasing power. Since Mr. and Mrs. X's objectives will cost more in the future, they will have to save more to realize their goals. For example, assuming an 8 percent return on their savings, Mr. and Mrs. X are no better off if hypothetically they have an average tax rate of 30 percent and inflation is 5.6 percent per year. Their real rate of return is zero.

$$
\begin{aligned}
\text{Real Rate of Return} &= \text{After Tax Rate of Return less Inflation} \\
&= 8\% - (30\% \times 8\%) - 5.6\% \\
&= 0\%
\end{aligned}
$$

Depending on their average tax rate, the rate of inflation and the length of time to fund their goals, Mr. and Mrs. X may have to save more than the amount indicated in Column 5.

14   Chapter 1

The Budget

Having determined their goals and the amounts needed to fund them, Mr. and Mrs. X can develop their budget. The budget period may cover an entire year but it could be more meaningful to break it into a series of monthly budgets which can then be combined to form a yearly budget.

The first step is to estimate income. *Estimated income* includes all anticipated receipts of money such as future salary, estimated profits (or losses which are deductions from income) from a business, bonuses, commissions, interest, dividends and gains. Mr. X earns a salary which means that payroll taxes will be withheld by his employer. These deductions can be shown in the income section or the expenditures section. Table 1.4 shows the estimated monthly income for Mr. and Mrs. X. Mr. X is expecting a raise of 8 percent for the coming year and Mrs. X expects her business to generate net profits of $36,000 for the year 1992.

Table 1.4   Budgeted Monthly Income for Mr. & Mrs. X

	Annual	Monthly Mr. X	Monthly Mrs. X	Combined
Mr. X's Gross Salary	$54,000	$4,500		
Less Withholdings:				
Federal Income Tax	(4,800)	(400)		
Social Security Tax	(4,131)	(344*)		
State Tax	(1,134)	(95*)		
Pension	(2,400)	(200)		
Life and Medical Insurance	(603)	(50*)		
Net Salary	40,932	3,411		$3,411
Mrs. X's Net Profits	36,000		$3,000	3,000
Interest and Dividends	4,800	200	200	400
Total Projected Net Income	$81,732	3,611	3,200	$6,811

* rounded to the nearest dollar.

Personal Financial Statements   15

The second step is to estimate all expenditures that will be made on a monthly basis. This should include a monthly amount for expenses such as insurance and real estate taxes that are paid annually or semiannually. Table 1.5 shows the projected budget, anticipating monthly income of $6,811 and estimated monthly expenditures of $4,967. The latter amount takes into account past expenditures plus any projected changes in the future.

Expenditures do not include the projected amounts needed to fund Mr. and Mrs. X's goals. Those amounts are added to the budget after the expenditures section. It is a good idea to incorporate goals into a budget because monthly income can then be set aside to address them. Since the first goal — to buy a new car — is short-term, the monthly amount of $2,000 is used. For other longer term goals, the time value of money is considered and amounts listed in Column 5 of Table 1.3 are used.

Since Mr. and Mrs. X's total monthly expenditures of $7,436 exceed planned monthly income of $6,811, there is a resultant deficit of $625 per month. This projected monthly deficit would equal an annual deficit of $7,494 that will be funded by withdrawals from cash. A surplus of income over expenditures will result in deposits to cash (Table 1.6).

1.6   Analysis of the Budget

Once the budget has been established, the next step is to analyze it. When Mr. and Mrs. X's goals are incorporated, they show a monthly deficit of $625 and a cumulative yearly deficit of $7,494 (12 × $625). The $6 difference is due to rounding. This deficit is the result of funding the X's first goal — to buy a new car in a year's time for $24,000. Can Mr. and Mrs. X afford this deficit?

Looking at their balance sheet (Table 1.1), Mr. and Mrs. X have $700 in checking accounts, $6,000 in savings and $7,000 in money market accounts from which to make withdrawals to cover this deficit. If Mr. and Mrs. X decide that they do not want to deplete their accounts, they could consider the following options:

- not to buy a new car; or

- buy a new car but extend the time to fund it; or

- look for ways to increase income and/or reduce expenditures.

If Mr. and Mrs. X decide to extend the date for buying a new car from twelve to eighteen months, the amount needed to fund this goal

16   Chapter 1

Table 1.5   Budget for Mr. & Mrs. X for 1992

	January		February		Annual	
	Budget	Actual	Budget	Actual	Budget	Actual
Total Income	$6,811		$6,811		$81,732	
Expenditures						
Food	568*		568		6,820	
Clothing	200		200		2,400	
Mortgages	738		738		8,860	
Utilities	188		188		2,250	
Home Insurance	50		50		600	
Life Insurance	317		317		3,800	
Medical, Dental	80		80		960	
Auto Loan	300		300		3,600	
Auto Maint., Ins.	217		217		2,600	
Real Estate Taxes	208		208		2,500	
Soc. Sec. Tax Mrs. X	459		459		5,508	
Estimated Taxes	600		600		7,200	
Contributions	167		167		2,000	
Recreation	167		167		2,000	
Summer Vacation	208		208		2,500	
Child Care	500		500		6,000	
Total	$4,967		$4,967		$59,598	
Goals						
Buy new car	2,000		2,000		24,000	
College fund	130*		130		1,560	
Retirement fund	201		201		2,412	
Living room furn.	138		138		1,656	
Total Expenditures	$7,436		$7,436		$89,226	
Surplus/(Deficit)	($625)		($625)		($7,494)	
Cash Deposit / (Withdrawal)	($625)		($625)		($7,494)	

* rounded to the nearest dollar.

Personal Financial Statements

Table 1.6 Budget for Mr. & Mrs. X for 1992

	January		February		Annual	
	Budget	**Actual**	**Budget**	**Actual**	**Budget**	**Actual**
Total Income	$6,811	$7,011	$6,811	$6,500	$81,732	
Expenditures						
Food	568*	580	568	550	6,820	
Clothing	200	170	200	210	2,400	
Mortgages	738	738	738	738	8,860	
Utilities	188	190	188	176	2,250	
Home Insurance	50	50	50	50	600	
Life Insurance	317	0	317	634	3,800	
Medical, Dental	80	0	80	150	960	
Auto Loan	300	300	300	300	3,600	
Auto Maint., Ins.	217	50	217	50	2,600	
Real Estate Taxes	208	208	208	208	2,500	
Soc. Sec. Tax Mrs. X	459	0	459	0	5,508	
Estimated Taxes	600	1,800	600	0	7,200	
Contributions	167	0	167	0	2,000	
Recreation	167	0	167	0	2,000	
Summer Vacation	208	0	208	450	2,500	
Child Care	500	500	500	500	6,000	
Total	$4,967	$4,586	$4,967	$4,016	$59,598	
Goals						
Buy new car	2,000	2,000	2,000	2,000	24,000	
College fund	130*	130	130	130	1,560	
Retirement fund	201	201	201	201	2,412	
Living room furn.	138	138	138	138	1,656	
Total Expenditures	$7,436	$7,055	$7,436	$6,485	$89,226	
Surplus/(Deficit)	($625)	($44)	($625)	$15	($7,494)	
Cash Deposit / (Withdrawal)	($625)	($44)	($625)	$15	($7,494)	

* rounded to the nearest dollar.

18   Chapter 1

will be reduced from $2,000 to $1,333 per month ($24,000/18 months). This would convert the deficit to a monthly surplus of $42.

Should Mr. and Mrs. X decide that they cannot wait that long to buy a new car, they could look for ways to cut proposed expenditures in their budget. Fixed expenditures are difficult to reduce but some discretionary items could be cut. Mr. and Mrs. X could forgo their summer vacation to save $2,500; reduce charitable contributions to save $2,000 and reduce recreational expenditures to save $2,000. These changes would reduce the cumulative deficit from $7,494 to a deficit of $994 (7,494 – 6,500).

The second form of budget analysis will be to compare actual income and expenditures with those budgeted. For example, in reviewing Mr. and Mrs. X's budget after the first two months into the new year (Table 1.6), significant differences between planned and actual expenditures should be investigated. Significant could be interpreted to mean differences over 5 percent to 10 percent.

For example, there are sizable variances between budgeted and actual expenditures in January and February for life insurance. Since Mr. and Mrs. X chose to pay their life insurance premiums every two months — or six times a year — no changes are needed. However, payments for auto insurance and maintenance of $50 for both January and February are much lower than the budgeted amount. Depending on how much is allocated for auto insurance, this expenditure could be reduced. Insignificant differences of less than 5 percent would not need to be investigated; larger discrepancies should be investigated and then changed.

The major objective of budget analysis is to find out if a surplus or deficit exists, why it has occurred and what corrective action could be taken.

Reviewing budgets on a monthly basis, although it requires more work, will give you a good feel for financial planning and help you to achieve the goals you have set by tailoring the budget to fit your needs.

Since budgeting is a repetitive process, using a personal computer can reduce some of the effort and save time. Many spreadsheet programs and software packages have been designed specifically for personal finance and can help in the preparation of your budget.

Your budget is an important link to the next accounting cycle because your actual yearly income and expenditures form the basis for the income statement for that year. The balance sheet should be updated to take care of any changes and a new budget should be formulated.

Lewis Carroll's *Alice in Wonderland* succinctly illustrates the importance of financial statements:

"Cheshire Puss" Alice began . . . "would you please tell me which way I ought to go from here?"

"That depends," said the cat, "on where you want to get to."

CHAPTER 2

PERSONAL AND FINANCIAL RECORD KEEPING

The key to compiling accurate and complete financial statements is the maintenance of adequate, orderly financial documents and records. Without an efficient system, you may not know what assets you have in order to compile your net worth. Adequate records should also be maintained for tax and insurance purposes for safety or security reasons or to establish a claim. Keeping complete records saves both time and money. If you don't have an important document on hand, for example, it may take time and some trouble to get a duplicate copy; an orderly record keeping system is well worth the effort.

2.1 What Records To Keep and Where To Keep Them

Documents and financial records can be stored at home, in a safe deposit box at a financial institution, or on your person. A safe deposit box provides the greatest security and should be used for your most important papers and valuables.

Storing records at home requires an orderly filing system. Stuffing papers into shoe boxes and envelopes may work initially but as more records are accumulated it becomes an exercise in futility when trying to locate a specific document. A file cabinet with storage folders offers an orderly convenient place to store records and documents. A metal filing cabinet is the most expensive but inexpensive cardboard filing cabinets will also serve the purpose. Major items such as bank statements, brokerage accounts, credit card statements, household information, savings and investments information, insurance policies and tax information should all have their own labeled folders and be filed alphabetically. Records and documents that are used often and can be replaced easily if lost can be kept at home. The purpose of an orderly filing system is to eliminate the wasted time involved in laboriously searching for documents and records by spending just a few minutes a week filing and retrieving documents.

21

Certain documents must be kept on your person: your driver's license, social security number, credit cards, health insurance information, etc.

The many different records you need can be easily organized into the following basic categories.

Personal Records

These include birth and marriage certificates, adoption papers, citizenship certificates, divorce decrees, military papers and all other documents pertaining to your life. These permanent records should be stored in a safe deposit box; photocopies can be kept in a home file.

Household and Automobile Records

Although this category involves many records, the most important are documents which convey ownership — deeds, in the case of a house,

Figure 2.1

condominium or real estate and title papers for automobiles. Since these papers are needed for resale and are difficult to replace if lost, they should be kept in a safe deposit box. A lease agreement if renting a house or apartment can be kept at home.

For tax purposes, homeowners should keep records of all expenditures made for home improvements because these add to the value of the house. This information is used to compute a gain (if any) for tax purposes when the house is sold. Section 2.2 contains additional information about tax records.

Automobile registration should be kept in your car but all maintenance and repair records should be kept in a home file. By keeping orderly service records, you can facilitate claims of problems which may have occurred while the car was still under warranty.

Bank, Savings and Investments

Your bank and savings accounts generate monthly bank statements with cancelled checks, savings statements, passbooks and certificates of deposit.

A separate folder for bank and savings accounts should be kept at home so that you will know how much money you have. Similarly, cancelled checks should be kept in a home folder because these represent receipts of payment. All tax-related cancelled checks should be put into your tax folder.

If savings certificates and certificates of deposit are kept in a safe deposit box for maximum security, records of the following information should be kept at home: the amount of the savings certificate or certificate of deposit, the date of maturity, the interest rate, the name of the financial institution and the certificate number. By having this information at hand, you can plan where to reinvest the money when the certificates mature. There is nothing to be gained by leaving your certificates of deposit with the financial institution after the maturity dates because they generally do not earn interest after these dates. It is important, therefore, to be aware of the maturity dates and the different investment alternatives to choose from for reinvestment.

Stocks and bonds are best kept in a safe deposit box even if they are in registered form (i.e., securities are registered in the name of the investor). As with certificates of deposit, accurate and complete records of your investments should be kept at home so that you can monitor their performance. Brokerage statements, confirmations of orders to buy and sell and a summary sheet with a record of all investments should be kept at home. See Table 2.1 for an example. If you have many different investments, it may be easier to use a summary sheet for each investment.

Table 2.1 Record of Investments

Description	Date of Purchase	Cost	Commission	Total Cost	Date of Sale	Amount Received
500 shares ABC Co. at $5.50	09/11/87	$2,750	$100	$ 2,850		
5 8% bonds XYZ Corp. at 99	10/15/88	4,950	250	5,200		
5000 shares equity mutual fund at $10.00	10/20/88	50,000	–	50,000		
400 shares equity mutual fund at $9.67	12/15/89	3,868	–	3,868		
				$61,918		

By keeping details of your investments, it is easy to review or change your strategies. Similarly, when selling any of your investments, your gain or loss (difference between proceeds from sale and the total cost) can be computed and this information can be transferred to your tax folder.

Credit Records

Credit contracts such as mortgages and home equity loans should be kept in a safe deposit box until they are paid off.

Loan payment, or coupon books, for mortgages and loans can be kept in a home file along with monthly credit card statements. Keep all charge card receipts and compare them to the amounts charged on your monthly statements.

By compiling a record of all of your loans, the amounts owed and monthly payment amounts, you can facilitate the preparation of your financial statements.

From a security point of view, it is wise to keep a list of all credit card numbers and telephone numbers of issuing financial institutions, in the event of theft or loss.

Insurance Records

All insurance policies (life, health, disability, accident, property liability, casualty, auto) should be kept in a home file so that they are easily accessible in the event of a claim. It is a good idea to list information about your insurance policies on a summary sheet and keep it in your safe deposit box with a copy in your home folder. See Table 2.2 for a sample summary sheet.

Insurance premiums need to be paid by their due dates, or the policies will expire. By keeping a record of the amounts and due dates on hand, it is easier to plan for these expenditures. Similarly, once this information has been compiled, it is easy to compare your coverage with that offered by competing insurance companies.

Consumer Purchases

For large ticket items, such as refrigerators and television sets, manufacturers usually provide warranties that should be kept in a home file until they expire. Service contracts should also be kept on file. Receipts of valuable items such as antiques, art and oriental rugs should be kept as long as you own the items. It is a good idea to keep photographs and

Table 2.2   Summary of Insurance Policies

Insurance	Company	Policy #	Insurance Coverage	Amount of Premium	Premium Due Date
Auto	Best Ins.	123456	500/500/100*	$1,200	July 1
Health	Blue Cross	234567		1,080	June 2
Disability	Best Ins.	345678	$2,000 per month	800	June 14
Home	Best Ins.	456789	$250,000	500	Aug. 14
Life	Next Life	567890	$200,000	1,400	Sept. 25
	Best Ins.	678901	$300,000	2,300	Feb. 15

* Liability limits.

professional appraisal values of valuables in your safe deposit box. In the event of a burglary or fire, it will be easier to file claims on these valuables if photographs and appraisal values can be produced.

An inventory list of your personal assets also helps you in the compilation of your balance sheet. Information to include on your list of personal assets is: the item, date of purchase, cost and the current fair market value. This list should be kept in a safe deposit box because if it is kept at home it could be reduced to ashes in a fire or destroyed in the event of a flood. A copy can be kept in a home file.

Retirement Plans

All information pertaining to pension plans, Keogh accounts, IRAs and SEP-IRAs should be kept in a folder in your filing cabinet. The monthly or quarterly statements of your pension accounts should be checked for accuracy concerning deposits by you or your employers, accumulations and withdrawals.

When you start receiving distributions from your retirement accounts, you will receive summary documents such as form 1099-R or W-2P which should be filed in your home tax folder.

Wills, Trusts and Estate Planning Information

Original copies of wills and trusts can be kept in a safe deposit box. It is important, however, to check your state laws governing the opening of the safe deposit box after an individual box holder's demise. Some states require a court order to open a safe deposit box which takes time to get and delays the payment of life insurance policies until the will or trust is obtained. Other states allow the spouse of the deceased to open the safe deposit box when the safe deposit box is rented jointly by the husband and wife. Some people opt to keep their original wills and trusts in a home file or with their attorneys. Your executor should be told the location of your original will and trust and a copy should be kept in your home file.

Although not imperative, it is advisable to compile various lists with a letter of your last instructions. This would include a list of your financial and personal assets and where they are kept, as well as a list of your liabilities. Included should be all of your bank accounts, savings accounts, mutual funds, certificates of deposit, the account numbers and names of the financial institutions and amounts in each account; the location of your life insurance policies, the location of your safe deposit box and where to find your real estate deeds and auto title papers; a list

28   Chapter 2

of stocks and bonds, the location of stock and bond certificates, or the name of the broker if they are held by the brokerage firm; the location of antiques, art, jewelry and other significant personal assets; mortgages with monthly amounts and other liabilities and the location of tax returns for previous years.

The second list should include the names, telephone numbers and addresses of family members and key financial advisors such as your accountant, lawyer, stockbroker, insurance agent and anyone else connected with your estate.

Preparing a letter of last instruction will assuredly not get top billing on your list of favorite activities but without one the executor of your estate may not know your last wishes. The letter should provide details of funeral arrangements, your wishes (if any) regarding organ transplants, distribution of personal assets such as jewelry, antiques, art, family heirlooms, etc. This letter can not be legally enforced if it disagrees in any way with the terms of your will but it can provide your executor and heirs with important information.

A copy of this letter and the two lists should be kept with the copy of your original will and/or trust. Duplicate copies of these can also be given to your executor, your attorney and stored in your safe deposit box.

Personal Financial Statements

Personal financial statements should be filed at home because they include all of the information affecting your financial status and are directly involved in financial planning. Copies of personal financial statements can also be stored in the folder with your will and estate information.

2.2   What Tax Records To Keep and How To Prepare for Your Accountant

There are many reasons why you should keep complete and orderly tax records. When you keep inclusive records of your income and deductions, you are able to prepare an accurate tax return. If your return is audited by the Internal Revenue Service (IRS), the orderly records you've kept can easily verify your deductions with a minimum of effort. (This, of course, won't prevail for any non-deductible items or highly questionable deductions you may have taken.) By keeping all-inclusive records of your expenses, you may be able to reduce the amount of income taxes you pay. If you *can't* prove your deductions because of sloppy record keeping, you may have to pay more income tax than necessary.

Copies of your tax returns should be kept in your home file as part of your tax records, with all records and receipts pertaining to income, deductions and credits that appear on your tax return. Table 2.3 lists the types of records to keep.

All the 1099-series of forms should be retained to support receipts of different types of income. Other records, such as brokerage statements and mutual fund statements that can prove the amounts of income shown on your tax return, should be kept in your folder.

Your checkbook and credit card statements provide basic records of your deductible expenditures. However, cancelled checks alone may not be sufficient evidence for the IRS, so you should also keep records of receipts and sales invoices. Dated and signed sales receipts are important if you pay cash.

Table 2.3   Tax Records to Keep

Income	Records
Wages and Salary	W-2 issued by employer
Independent Contractor	1099-Misc issued by the entity you have provided services for
Business Income-proprietorship, partnership, estates, trusts, S-corporations, rents, royalties	Business books, K-1 issued by partnerships
Interest and Dividends	1099-Int and 1099-Div issued by the financial institutions paying the interest and dividends
Capital Gains and Losses	1099-B issued by broker who sold the assets. 1099-S issued by broker reporting proceeds on sale of real estate
State and Local Tax Refunds	1099-G issued by state or local government that has provided the refund
Payments/Distributions from Retirement plans and annuities	1099-R or W-2P issued by the trustee of the plan making the payment
Social Security Benefits	SSA-1099 issued by the federal government
Unemployment Compensation	1099-G issued by government agency paying the unemployment compensation
Barter Income	1099-B issued when services or properties are exchanged

(Table continues)

30   Chapter 2

Table 2.3   Continued

Expenditures	Records
Medical & Dental Expenses	cancelled checks and receipts
Taxes	cancelled checks and receipts for real estate taxes, personal property taxes, state and local taxes, etc.
Interest	1098 issued by mortgage company, cancelled checks and receipts for deductible interest
Contributions	cancelled checks and receipts from donees
Miscellaneous Deductions	cancelled checks and receipts
Business use of auto, home	cancelled checks, receipts and documentation
Alimony	cancelled checks, copy of divorce decree or separation agreement

How To Prepare for Your Accountant

Many people meet with an accountant at least once a year to prepare their income tax returns. By organizing and summarizing your tax information ahead of time, you can save your accountant considerable time which should cut the costs of preparing your tax return.

By organizing and summarizing your information, you can do the "legwork" rather than have your accountant plow through your receipts, cancelled checks and other documentation. If, however, your accountant requests your supporting documentation, you will be able to provide it.

Your summary sheet should show your name, name of spouse (if applicable), address, telephone number, social security number(s), marital status, names of dependents (if applicable), social security numbers of children and their dates of birth. List all sources of income as shown in the example in Table 2.4.

As you can see from the example, Mr. and Mrs. Y have many sources of interest, dividend income and capital gains, which are summarized in the schedule. If your financial activities have not changed very much since last year, your prior year's tax return is a good source to check to see if you have omitted any sources of income.

The Internal Revenue Service crosschecks your reported income with the documentation it receives from reporting institutions, corpora-

Personal and Financial Record Keeping   31

You should give your accountant your W-2 forms which are then attached to your filed federal, state and local tax returns. Similarly, if you have changed accountants, give your new accountant copies of your prior year's tax returns.

If your deductions exceed the amount of the standard allowable deduction, you may choose to itemize your deductible expenses. By organizing and summarizing your deductible expenses, you will save your accountant time and yourself money. Table 2.5 shows a worksheet whereby checks of deductible expenses are sorted and summarized. If you are not sure which expenses are deductible, check with your accountant.

Your accountant may ask you to fill out a checklist or questionnaire so that all relevant information is obtained. The aim of working closely with your accountant is to prepare an accurate tax return and not overpay your taxes.

2.3   How Long To Keep Records

There are no simple answers as to how long tax records should be kept. If there is any under reporting of income, or if a return is fraudulent, the Internal Revenue Service can delve back many, many years and ask you to substantiate or support your income and deductions.

Generally, however, tax records must be kept for at least three years from the date that the federal income tax return was filed or two years from the date that the tax was paid, whichever is later. If there is under reported income greater than 25 percent of income reported on the return, records must be kept six years after the return was filed.

If a return is fraudulent or false, records should be kept indefinitely. The same applies if no return is filed.

Certain tax records should be kept longer than the period of limitations: records showing the date, cost and proceeds of sale of property, improvements made to property, purchase of stocks, bonds, mutual funds and records showing contributions to non-deductible IRAs.

All other records can accumulate to overwhelming numbers and you will want to get rid of some documents from time to time. There are certain records such as birth certificates, marriage licenses and divorce decrees that should be kept permanently.

Bank statements, credit card statements, investment records and cancelled checks should be kept for at least three years and, if related to your taxes, a longer period of time. Expired insurance policies, warranties and service contracts can be thrown out.

The purpose of storing records systematically is to enable easy retrieval of any record that is required. Both members of a married couple

32   Chapter 2

Table 2.4   Income Tax Summary

| John H. Y | Date of Birth: June 2, 1956 | Social Security #: 000-00-0000 |
| Mary C. Y | Date of Birth: June 7, 1957 | Social Security #: 000-00-0000 |

Marital Status: Married

Children:
| David | Date of Birth: June 3, 1985 | Social Security #: 000-00-0000 |
| Lisa | Date of Birth: June 4, 1989 | Social Security #: 000-00-0000 |

Source of Income

Salary: John's W-2

Gross	Fed. With.	Soc. Sec. Tax	State Tax	City Tax
$50,000	$7,200	$3,825	$1,050	$2,156

Business Income: Mary from Business Books

$40,000

Refund of State Tax: $120

Interest Income		Dividend Income	
Forever S&L	$ 15	Vanguard Corp	$215
Ace Bank	450	Welcome Corp	25
Fail Safe Bank	375	Ajax Corp	200
	$840	Scattergood Co.	40
		Barlow Corp	15
			$495

Capital Gains:

	Proceeds	Date of Sale	Date of Purchase	Cost
Sold 100 shares ABC Corp for	$10,100	06/15/90	01/04/89	5,600
Sold 50 shares Mutual Fund	500	07/10/90	01/14/88	550

Sale of Home:

Date of Purchase and Cost of Old House	April 15, 1978	$ 75,000
Improvements		20,000
Selling Expenses		6,000
Proceeds and Date of Sale	June 15, 1990	94,000
Date of Purchase and Cost of New House	June 15, 1990	150,000

Table 2.5 Worksheet: Check Analysis of Deductible Expenses

John and Mary Y - 1990

Check #	Date	Payee	Amount	Taxes	Medical	Interest	Contributions	Other
215	1/15	F.A.S. Bee, CPA	200 00					200 00
216	1/15	State-Personal Property Tax	39 00	39 00				
230	2/10	Dr. B. Well	80 00		80 00			
231	2/10	Ds. P.D. Rad	90 00		90 00			
256	3/5	Church-Temple Donation	200 00				200 00	
270	4/20	Super Quick Motors-Auto	187 00					187 00
291	5/08	Fail Safe Bank-Personal Interest	150 00			150 00		
296	5/30	Central School-Child Care	500 00					500 00
315	4/15	IRS 1040 ES	750 00	750 00				
316	4/15	State Estimated Payment	150 00	150 00				
325	7/20	State Bank-Safe Deposit Box	40 00					40 00
380	8/29	Go Moving Company	2000 00					2000 00
399	9/15	IRS 1040 ES	750 00	750 00				
400	9/15	State Estimated Payment	150 00	150 00				
450	9/30	SPCA-Donation	50 00					50 00
490	12/6	Best Auto Insurance	500 00					500 00
		Sub Totals	5836 00	1839 00	170 00	150 00	200 00	3477 00
		From W2						
		State Tax	1050 00	1050 00				
		City Tax	2156 00	2156 00				
		From 1098						
		Real Estate Tax	2100 00	2100 00				
		Mortgage Interest	5001 00			5001 00		
		TOTALS	16143 00	7145 00	170 00	5151 00	200 00	3477 00

34   Chapter 2

should be familiar with the filing system, records involved and above all, their financial affairs.

2.4   How To Reconcile Your Checking Account

Believe it or not, many people never even open their monthly checking account statements and some adjust their accounts to whatever the bank balance is. There are also those who reconcile their accounts to the last cent. If you are not part of the latter group, you might ask: why bother?

By reconciling your account, you can adjust for any bank charges or interest added, errors made by you or the bank (banks are not infallible, they do occasionally make errors) to come up with your corrected account balance.

This author once made a deposit only to find upon examination of the monthly bank statement that the bank had not credited it to her account. Thus, her balance fell below the minimum balance required for free checking, resulting in the bank charging check fees. A letter was promptly sent with a copy of the deposit slip to the bank and they credited her account and rescinded the check fees.

The starting point in reconciling your checking account is to examine your monthly checking account statement. The bank statement will show the deposits that have been credited and the checks that have cleared the account for the monthly period. The ending date of the statement may or may not coincide with the last day of the month. Banks spread their workload of generating monthly statements evenly throughout the monthly period. Table 2.6 shows a monthly bank statement for John Y.

Included with your monthly bank statement are cancelled checks. Checks that have cleared the bank should be marked off (✔) as has been done in Mr. Y's checkbook in Table 2.7. Checks not marked with a (✔) are outstanding and have not cleared Mr Y's account as of the statement date.

Figure 2.2 shows a copy of a cancelled check which was written for $1,200 but comparing the last six digits encoded on the bottom right hand corner of the check, we see that the bank charged the account $1,201. By presenting copies of this cancelled check and the bank statement to the bank, they will reimburse the account for the difference charged. By marking off cancelled checks against your checkbook register, you are not only establishing which checks are still outstanding, you are also confirming that the bank has charged the correct amount for each check written.

To reconcile your account you need to identify six components:

Table 2.6   Monthly Bank Statement

EVERLASTING BANK
1 Sparkle Circle
Somewhere, USA

John Y
1 Upbeat Place
Somewhere, USA   Account #: 000-00000

Previous Statement Date	1/31/90	Balance		$2,140.57
Deposits and other credits		4 transactions		3,082.87
Checks and other debits		15 transactions		2,379.10
Ending Balance	2/28/90			2,844.34

Date	Check#	Debits	Credits	Balance
2/1				$2,140.57
2/2	343	20.00	2,906.37	5,026.94
2/5	356	1,201.00		3,825.94
2/6	357	56.14		3,769.80
2/9	359	91.12	25.00	3,703.68
2/12	361	150.00		3,553.68
2/14	362	221.50		3,332.18
2/16	363	87.20		3,244.98
2/20	365	200.00		3,044.98
	366	26.00		3,018.98
2/21	367	15.36	150.00	3,153.62
2/23	368	76.12		3,077.50
	369	150.00		2,927.50
2/24	370	56.06		2,871.41
2/28	373	23.50		2,847.94
2/28		5.10SC	1.50IN	2,844.34

DM   Debit Memo   SC   Service Charge   FC   Finance Charge   IN   Interest

36   Chapter 2

Table 2.7   Mr. Y's Checkbook Register

NUMBER	DATE 1990	DESCRIPTION OF TRANSACTION	PAYMENT/DEBIT (-)		√ T	FEE (IF ANY) (-)	DEPOSIT/CREDIT (+)		BALANCE $2120 57	
356	2·1	Complete Financial Service	$1200	00	√	$	$		1200	
									920	57
	2·2	Deposit			√		2906	37	2906	37
									3826	94
357	2·3	Bell Telephone	56	14	√				56	14
									3770	80
358	2·4	Electric Company	124	16					124	16
									3646	64
359	2·5	EZ Food Market	91	12	√				91	12
									3555	52
	2·9	Deposit - Forever S&L Dividend			√		25	00	25	00
									3580	52
360	2·10	Ace Insurance Company	650	00					650	00
									2930	52
361	2·11	Cash	150	00	√				150	00
									2780	52
362	2·12	Leak Free Roofers	221	50	√				221	50
									2559	02
363	2·15	EZ Food Market	87	20	√				87	20
									2471	82
364	2·16	Animal Hospital	35	00					35	00
									2436	82
365	2·17	Last County Bank	200	00	√				200	00
									2236	82
366	2·18	Kroft Pharmacy	26	00	√				26	00
									2210	82
367	2·19	First Bookstore	$ 15	36	√	$	$		15	36
									2195	46
	2·20	Deposit - Seave Brokerage Dividend			√		150	00	150	00
									2345	46
368	2·21	Gas Company	76	12	√				76	12
									2269	34
369	2·21	Cash	150	00	√				150	00
									2119	34
370	2·22	EZ Food Market	56	06	√				56	06
									2063	25
371	2·23	Playful Toy Store	23	25					23	25
									2040	03
372	2·24	Numero Uno Department Store	45	00					45	00
									1995	03
373	2·27	EZ Food Market	23	50	√				23	50
									1971	53
	2·28	Deposit					2906	37	2906	37
									4877	90

Personal and Financial Record Keeping   37

Figure 2.2

- ending balance in your bank statement;
- ending balance in your check register for the same period;
- bank charges and service fees;
- interest earned;
- deposits in transit;
- outstanding checks.

Mr. Y's check register (Table 2.7) shows an ending balance of $4,877.90 on February 28, whereas the bank shows an ending monthly balance of $2,844.34.

Checks outstanding are:

#	Amount
358	$ 124.16
360	650.00
364	35.00
371	23.25
372	45.00
	$877.41

38   Chapter 2

There is one deposit in transit which is the deposit on February 28 for $2,906.37, which the bank has, as of the statement date, not credited to Mr. Y's account.

Begin with the checkbook balance as of the closing date of the monthly statement, add any interest earned and deduct the bank charges and fees.

Balance per checkbook	$ 4,877.90
less: service charge	(5.10)
add: interest earned	1.50
Adjusted checkbook balance	$ 4,874.30

The adjusted bank balance is computed as follows:

Start with the ending bank balance for the month, add any deposits in transit and deduct the outstanding checks.

Balance per bank	$ 2,844.34
add: deposits in transit	2,906.37
less: checks outstanding	(877.41)
	4,873.30
add: bank error (check #356 written for $1200.00, bank charged $1201.00)	1.00
Adjusted bank balance	$ 4,874.30

If the adjusted balances are not the same, there is an error. The following sequence of steps can be used to find the error, starting with the first step and progressing until the error is found:

1. Confirm that you have included all the outstanding checks and that they are correctly added.
2. Check that you have included all the deposits in transit.
3. Check your bank statement to see that you have included all the bank charges and interest earned.
4. Recheck the addition and subtraction in your check register.
5. Recheck the amounts written on the cancelled checks with the amounts written in your check register.
6. Recheck the amounts written on the cancelled checks with the coded digits on the bottom right hand corner of the checks.

If you still have not found the error, it is more than likely that you are overlooking something which is obvious. Leave it for a while and then come back to it.

Although the example used has only a small number of checks, the method is the same for reconciling checking accounts with greater numbers of checks written and deposits made.

By reconciling your checking account monthly, you are confirming that your checking account balance is what it should be and you are safely guarding an important asset — your cash.

In these first two chapters, the tools of basic personal finance are presented to help you assess your financial situation. The following chapters concentrate on ways to better manage your money and financial wealth through an understanding of the underlying concepts of personal finance.

Chapter 3
HOW TO SAVE MONEY

You have two choices to make concerning your income—spend it or save it. If you decide to save it, you face the problem (a nice problem though—there can be a lot worse than this!) of where to invest your money. Alternatives range from putting money under the mattress, leaving it in a checking account earning little or no interest, buying stocks and bonds, speculating in copper futures in the hopes of trebling your investment in a short period of time to gambling at the tables in a casino. Some investments will produce substantial profits, some substantial losses, others will earn meager returns.

Making sense of the staggering number of investment choices is important for the saver because money invested now is the bridge to future purchasing power. You must choose the investments to include in your portfolio that can provide you with future wealth. A poor choice of investments or poor management of them can result in the liquidation of these assets and no future accumulation of wealth. Determining which investments to choose for a portfolio will depend on several factors such as your goals or objectives, the level of risk involved, the rate of return, rate of inflation, tax factors and liquidity considerations.

3.1 Savings Objectives

Savings objectives vary from individual to individual and often change over the years. Such objectives are important because they determine the purpose of your investment portfolio. Your objectives might include: accumulating wealth for retirement; funding your children's education; preparation for financial emergencies; providing for a large estate; accumulating a specific amount of money.

Clearly your stage in the family life cycle influences the setting of objectives. A young family with small children will have objectives that differ greatly from a couple ready to retire and the mix of assets in the respective portfolios will also be very different. A young couple's portfolio can hold growth stocks and long-term bonds whereas the portfolio of a couple close to retirement would stress assets with assured returns and a higher proportion of assets which can easily be converted into cash.

41

Figure 3.1 Relationships Between Objectives and Investment Plans

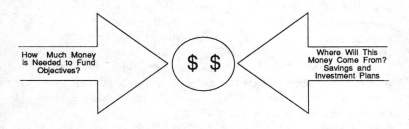

You will have both short-range and long-range objectives; short-range objectives are much easier to pursue. However, you can coordinate these objectives by assigning priorities to them and quantifying the amount of future dollars that will be needed to fund them (this can be done with the help of an accountant, financial planner, lawyer, banker, etc.). This is illustrated in Chapter One. A comprehensive investment plan can then be designed to allocate savings to different investments to achieve these objectives. Your investment plan should consider the following factors:

- the level of risk;
- the rate of return;
- the level of inflation;
- the tax situation;
- liquidity and marketability.

The Level of Risk

Once you have set your objectives, determine the level of risk that can be assumed. For example, investing in interest rate futures and oil and gas limited partnerships may offer you greater returns (if the investments are successful) than if you were to invest in U.S. Treasury bills. However, if the interest rate futures and/or the limited partnerships go sour, you may lose part or all of your invested capital. With Treasury bills, a certain return (in addition to the invested capital) is assured if you hold the bills to maturity.

Risk is the uncertainty related to the outcome of the investment and all investments involve risk. Treasury bills with an assured return from the government are less risky than interest rate futures that may double your money or lose your entire investment. This does not mean that you should retreat to Treasury bills or stashing money under the mattress; these actions also have their risks. There are six major categories of risk and you should be aware of how they affect different investments.

Business Risk refers to the nature of a company. Some companies are riskier than others, and investing in their stocks and bonds increases the risk of loss. If a company goes bankrupt, the common stockholders and unsecured bondholders may lose their entire investment. Business risk can be reduced by investing in companies that are financially sound and have products with strong consumer demand.

Financial Risk refers to the amount of debt a company has in relation to its equity. The greater the debt-to-equity ratio, the higher the financial risk, because the company will have to make fixed commitments of interest payments and repayments of principal. Failure of a company to meet its commitments can lead it to bankruptcy. Companies with very little or no debt will obviously have very little or no financial risk. Financial risk can be reduced by investing in companies which have low debt to equity ratios.

Political Risk refers to the changes in the environment which affect a company's operations. For example, government intervention in the private sector, currency devaluations, changes in government and tax changes, could affect a company's profits. Companies in Hong Kong, for example, face political risks due to the termination of the British lease when "ownership" of Hong Kong reverts back to mainland China. Since political events often occur overnight or with very little warning, it may be difficult for investors to anticipate which companies will be adversely affected. It is easier to avoid investing in companies in troubled countries such as Iran, Iraq, Lebanon, etc., than to anticipate political changes to the environments in the industrialized nations.

Interest Rate Risk refers to the changes in market rates of interest which affect all investments. Fixed income securities are most directly affected. When market rates of interest change, fixed income securities change, increasing in price when interest rates decrease and decreasing in price when interest rates increase. Thus, in periods of rising interest

44   Chapter 3

rates, investors who hold fixed income securities will find that their market prices will fall because investors want a competitive yield. Similarly, in periods of declining interest rates, prices of these fixed income securities will rise. The interest rate risk may be lessened by investing in fixed income securities with different maturities — the longer the term to maturity, the greater the interest rate risk.

Market Risk refers to the movement of asset prices (such as art, real estate, stamps, stocks, etc.) which tend to move together. When the stock market rises, most stocks go up in price, including those with less than spectacular sales, growth and earnings. Similarly, when the stock market declines, so do most of the individual stocks including those with better than average sales, growth and earnings. These stock price fluctuations may not have anything to do with how well or badly the companies are doing. Market risk is caused by external factors such as economic, political and social factors. It may be difficult to avoid market risk since it affects all assets with fluctuating prices. With all these risks encompassing so many investments, you may feel that the only avenue left to avoid risk and ensure a good nights sleep is to put money under the mattress. That, too, is subject to risk — purchasing power risk.

Purchasing Power Risk refers to the changes in price levels in the economy and affects all investments. During periods of rising prices, known as inflation, there is a loss of purchasing power (the ten-cent candy bar of my youth which now costs close to $1). With inflation, there is the risk that your future dollars will have their buying power eroded. Purchasing power risk has the greatest effect on investments that have fixed returns (bonds, savings accounts) and no returns (noninterest-bearing checking accounts and of course, the hoard under the mattress). Assets whose values move with general price levels, such as common stocks and real estate, do much better during periods of moderate inflation than do fixed income securities. In order to better combat purchasing power risk, aim for a portfolio of assets whose rate of return exceeds that of anticipated inflation.

It is evident that risk cannot be avoided even when investing in the most conservative investments — savings accounts and U.S. Treasury bills. Certain levels of risk can be minimized, however, through diversification — the opposite of putting all of your eggs in one basket. Rather than investing everything in the stock of one company, you could invest in several companies. You can also diversify by buying different types of securities such as bonds, stocks and government securities. Diversification is often difficult to achieve if you have only a small amount of money to invest.

It is important to understand and recognize the various levels of risk so that they can be minimized in the construction of an investment

How To Save Money   45

portfolio. There is a direct relationship between risk and return; you are compensated with greater returns for accepting greater risks. In most situations, investing in stocks with the greatest rate of return and the greatest risk, does not lead to wealth — it may lead only to financial disaster.

The Rate of Return

Investors invest in assets in order to earn a return which may be in the form of income (interest and dividends) and/or capital appreciation (when the price of the asset rises between the time of purchase and sale). Some investments, such as savings accounts and U.S. Treasury bills, offer only income with no capital appreciation, while others such as common stocks — which do not pay dividends — offer the potential for capital appreciation. Of course, if these stocks go down in value, there will be capital losses. The total return would include both income and capital gains/losses where applicable. Calculating a return is important because it is a measure of the growth or decline of your wealth. At different intervals, the asset portfolio would be evaluated as to the rate of return earned against the investor's objectives.

The rate of return is expressed as a percentage and can be calculated as follows:

$$\text{Rate of Return} \quad = \quad \frac{(\text{Ending value} - \text{Beginning value}) + \text{Income}}{\text{Gross Purchase Price}}$$

It is important to deduct any fees or commissions charged. For example, if a share of common stock was purchased at the beginning of the year for $50 and sold at the end of the year for $70, with a commission of $2 charged at each end (for purchase and sale), and a $2 dividend was paid, the rate of return is 44 percent, as calculated below:

$$\text{Rate of Return} \quad = \quad \frac{(\$68 - 48) + 2}{50}$$
$$= \quad 44\%$$

The return will depend on several factors such as the type of investment, the period of time involved and the levels of risk. Dr. Roger Ibottson (1985) supervised a study comparing rates of return earned by different types of securities over the sixty-year period from 1926. His conclusions were that the greatest rates of return were earned by common stocks of small companies (arithmetic mean rate of return of 18.2 percent) which also had the greatest risk (standard deviation of 36.3 percent), followed by common stocks of both large and small companies with

46   Chapter 3

lower rates of return (11.7 percent) and risk (21.2 percent). Next were
corporate bonds (return 4.4 percent and risk 7.6 percent), then long-term
government bonds (return 3.7 percent and risk 7.5 percent) and then U.S.
Treasury bills with the lowest rate of return (3.3 percent) and risk (3.3
percent).

This does not mean that by buying small company stocks you are
automatically guaranteed the highest rates of return. The standard deviation of 36.3 percent indicates the greatest variability of returns and thus
is the riskiest. This is well illustrated with the stock market highs and
lows: if someone who has invested in the stock market needs the money
at a time when the market is down, a loss will be suffered since the
investor cannot wait for the market to rebound.

The Level of Inflation

Inflation has been around and will continue to be around in the financial
environment; every effort should be made to protect yourself from
unanticipated price increases. The rate of inflation or anticipated inflation
should be included in the construction of assets in a portfolio with regard
to their rate of return. For example, if the rate of inflation is anticipated
at 4 percent, the required rates of return on Treasury bills, bonds and
other fixed income securities would have to increase to include this
erosion of future purchasing power. Thus, the real rate of return on
Treasury bills yielding 6 percent per annum would be 2 percent (6 percent
– 4 percent inflation rate). If inflation rises during this period to more
than 6 percent, a negative real rate of return will occur.

Unanticipated inflation will have a greater impact on long-term
debt securities (corporate and government bonds). Market prices of
existing bonds will go down in order to make their market rates of return
more competitive (to include the rate of inflation). Existing bondholders
who have invested in long-term bonds will see the market price of their
bonds tumble and the interest that they receive may not cover the rate
of inflation (anticipated plus unanticipated). Other types of investments
such as stocks and real estate, have historically done better against
inflation.

The Tax Situation

When choosing portfolio investments, it is important to consider your
tax situation since different investments are not taxed in the same way.
This is particularly important in the higher tax brackets. Both income
and capital gains are taxed at the federal and state levels; at the local

level, some counties assess personal property taxes on the value of investors' portfolios. Investors with high levels of income, as well as large tax preference items and adjustments may be subjected to an additional tax (on the federal income tax return) called the *alternative minimum tax.*

As taxes are levied on income and capital gains, the after tax rates of return of different investments must be compared. The after tax rate of return is calculated as:

Rate of Return (after tax) = (1 − tax rate)Rate of Return (before taxes)

For example, a corporate bond yielding 10 percent to an investor with a marginal tax rate of 28 percent has an after tax rate of return of 7.2 percent:

$$R = (1 - .28).10$$

This can be compared with the rate of return of a municipal bond which is tax free at the federal level. In many cases, taxes will affect the choice of investments and effective tax planning may reduce the amount of taxes paid.

Liquidity and Marketability

You must carefully consider your situation with regard to the liquidity and marketability of investments in your portfolio. *Liquidity* is the ability to be able to convert your investment into cash without losing a significant amount of the funds invested.

The ability to be able to sell an investment quickly refers to its *marketability*. When investing funds which are to be used in a short period of time, you would need to invest in assets which are high in liquidity (savings accounts, certificates of deposit, Treasury bills). If, however, your goals are long-term — saving for retirement in twenty years, for example — marketability becomes more important than liquidity. In this case, you could invest in assets such as quality common stocks, investment grade corporate bonds, Treasury bonds, municipal bonds, etc. These are all readily marketable in that they can be sold in the secondary markets (major stock exchanges and bond exchanges). These investments offer the potential for income and growth and also future convertibility into cash. Stocks of growth and speculative companies and high yielding bonds may be less marketable as well as having greater risks (business and financial) regarding future convertibility into cash.

All investment assets have different characteristics and varying levels of risk, return, tax status, liquidity and marketability. To make the

48   Chapter 3

appropriate choices of investments for your portfolio, you must understand these characteristics.

3.2   Investor Guidelines

The following examples are guidelines to be followed at different stages in the family life cycle.

Keep a certain amount of funds in liquid assets (such as money market mutual funds, passbook savings and Treasury bills) to meet emergencies. How much to keep in liquid assets will vary according to your individual circumstances; conservatively, keep three to six months worth of expenses in liquid assets.

The balance (after deducting the amount left in liquid assets) could be invested in different types of assets depending on where you are in the family life cycle.

These are *suggestions* , not rules; everyone's situation differs. (See Table 3.1 for a summary of the guidelines of investment plans for different types of investors).

Single Investor

If you are a single investor with no dependents and enough income to set aside savings, the following investment plan and objectives may work for you:

- Short-term objectives: to set aside a portion of savings in liquid assets for emergencies.

- Medium-term objectives: to set aside funds to buy a condominium or starter home.

- Long-term objectives: to set aside funds for retirement.

A portfolio for a single investor with no dependents would favor assets returning future growth and capital gains over current income. The levels of risk tolerance vary: if you have small amounts of money to invest, you can't take investment risks as large as someone with large amounts of money. Assets offering growth are common stocks of companies that pay little or no dividends but use their earnings to finance their growth and expansion (it is important to differentiate between growth oriented companies and speculative high risk companies), common stock mutual funds, real estate, convertible securities, and on the more speculative side, options, precious metals and partnerships. Types

| | How To Save Money | 49 |

Table 3.1	Table of Portfolio Guidelines			
	Single Investor	**Young Married Couple**	**Older Married Couple**	**Retirement**
Portfolio Size: To $50,000				
Cash	25%	20%	15%	10%
Equities	50%	50%	35%	20%
Real Estate	0%	10%	10%	10%
Convertibles	10%	5%	10%	0%
Fixed Income	15%	10%	25%	60%
Speculative	0%	5%	5%	0%
Total	100%	100%	100%	100%
Portfolio Size: To $100,000				
Cash	15%	15%	10%	10%
Equities	50%	50%	35%	30%
Real Estate	10%	10%	10%	5%
Convertibles	10%	10%	5%	5%
Fixed Income	10%	10%	30%	50%
Speculative	5%	5%	10%	0%
Total	100%	100%	100%	100%
Portfolio Size: To $250,000				
Cash	10%	10%	10%	10%
Equities	55%	50%	30%	20%
Real Estate	15%	15%	10%	10%
Convertibles	5%	10%	10%	10%
Fixed Income	10%	10%	30%	50%
Speculative	5%	5%	10%	0%
Total	100%	100%	100%	100%
Portfolio Size: To $1,000,000				
Cash	10%	10%	10%	10%
Equities	50%	35%	20%	15%
Real Estate	20%	20%	20%	15%
Convertibles	5%	10%	10%	10%
Fixed Income	10%	15%	30%	50%
Speculative	5%	10%	10%	0%
Total	100%	100%	100%	100%

50   Chapter 3

of assets vary with the size of the portfolio, the time available to manage the portfolio and the knowledge of the different types of investments.

A small portfolio, for example, might include a portion in liquid assets and the rest in common stock mutual funds. A large portfolio might include investments in all the categories mentioned. However, if you do not have the time available to manage the investments, it may be more prudent to invest in common stock mutual funds than individual common stocks. It is important to be knowledgeable about the types of investments you make. Avoid investing in assets which you do not understand.

Young Married Couple

If you are a young married couple with dependent children, your objectives may be:

- Short-term: to set aside savings to obtain enough capital for life and disability insurance and for emergencies.

- Short-term to medium-term: to buy a home.

- Long-term: to set aside funds for retirement and to build an estate.

The priorities of the investment plan would be to provide protection for dependents through life insurance. The object is to provide enough income for dependents to live on in the event of the demise of the "breadwinners." Disability insurance is equally important because it protects against the loss of the breadwinners' salaries due to injury or illness. Buying a home has important advantages, namely tax deductibility of the mortgage interest and real estate taxes and the ability to build equity in the house. However, in the strictest sense, buying a home is not a true investment. Whatever money is left to invest should be put into assets which offer future growth such as common stocks of growth companies, common stock mutual funds and real estate. If you have money to invest, knowledge of the level of risk involved and can withstand the risk of speculation, you could consider precious metals, convertible securities, options, etc.

Older Married Couple

At this stage, you've probably settled into a job, profession or business and are at the peak of your earnings. Your children may either be entering college or have left the nest. Most financial obligations may be close to being paid off. Your objectives may be:

- Short-term: to set aside savings for adequate life insurance and commitments.

- Medium-term to long-term: to set aside funds for retirement and build an estate.

Priorities of the investment plan would include aggressively building up assets for retirement and an estate, particularly if large amounts of cash are available for investing. Tax considerations may make investing in municipal bonds, tax-deferred plans and tax shelters more attractive. In order to obtain portfolio growth, you may have the bulk of your assets invested in common stocks, common stock mutual funds, real estate and the more speculative investments. Actual portfolios will vary significantly due to the differences in investor's income, level of knowledge, level of risk and family situation.

Retirement

Upon reaching retirement, your objectives might be:

- Short-term: to set aside savings for adequate life and health insurance.

- Short-term to medium-term: to allocate portfolio assets to provide investment income.

- Long-term: to provide for a long retirement and an estate.

When nearing retirement, you will need to be more conservative regarding risk. Investment priorities usually involve generating income that will provide financial independence and security. Although some retiring investors may want to sell any investments that require their time, knowledge and effort to manage (partnerships, business interests and real estate) — others may want to become actively involved in these endeavors in retirement. The makeup of your portfolio would favor at least half the assets being invested in fixed income securities, blue-chip common stocks, or equity income mutual funds and real estate. Depending on individual circumstances, tax considerations may be important: tax-deferred annuities and single premium life insurance policies may reduce your current tax liability. As the value of your estate increases, tax saving strategies become an even more important part of estate planning.

52　　　Chapter 3

To summarize, quantify the amount needed for each of your objectives and add 5-10 percent for inflation each year. Using 10 percent inflation, you will need 10 percent more in income each year. With these future amounts, you can work out how much you will need to save in the present, at the assumed rate of returns of the various investment assets, to generate this future sum.

Select specific investments for each of the financial objectives so that there is an adequate mix of liquid versus nonliquid investments.

Determine the level of risk tolerance that makes you comfortable. This level may be reevaluated up or down as circumstances change. Generally, the level of risk tolerance increases with increasing wealth, liquidity and knowledge of investments, decreasing as you near retirement age. You should decide on a reasonable balance of risk and return, bearing in mind that greater risk may increase the return and also increase the risk of loss. Diversification of investments can help you achieve the greatest level of returns for the amount of risk that you are willing to bear.

Revise investment alternatives as circumstances change. Never invest in something which you do not understand. If someone else is administering your portfolio, make it your business to understand and follow up on the investment choices. There have been too many incidents of portfolio mismanagement involving administrators who have been more concerned with excessive trading than the long-term steady growth of portfolios. If you decide not to manage your own portfolio, carefully investigate the track record of any individual or organization you may choose to administer your holdings. Discuss their investment philosophies and make sure you feel confident and comfortable with them before employing their services.

Evaluate your investment portfolio periodically with regard to the characteristics of the investments (risk, return, diversification, inflation, tax situation, liquidity and marketability) and your financial condition. Make sure that your investment plan relates to your goals and objectives and allows you to achieve them. Goals may change and require changes in your investment plan and portfolio. In order to adapt to the changes in your financial plan, always be aware of your financial resources in order to know how much you can save.

CHAPTER 4

HOW TO READ THE FINANCIAL PAGES

A wealth of confusing information appears in the financial pages of the newspapers. Terms like *CPI, GNP, S & P 500 Index, Ml, M2, M3, short interest*, etc., are bandied about as if they were codes to a secret society. Often the same data is used by different economists and financial analysts to arrive at different conclusions about the state of the world's economy and financial markets.

This is not unlike what happens when several doctors examine one patient. The performance of different tests may lead to varying diagnoses and the patient is closely watched for signs leading to definitive diagnoses. Similarly, financial analysts study different statistical measures and indicators to provide more information about the directions in which the economy and financial markets are headed.

The clearest picture of the economy and financial markets is presented, of course, through hindsight — too late for investment decisions. By interpreting economic and market indicators, investors are looking for early warnings of anticipated changes in the direction of the stock and bond markets. On the other hand, if economists and financial analysts can't agree on the state of the markets of the economy, how can individual investors know where to turn for definitive answers?

It isn't that important for you to understand all of the nuances of economic forecasts — what is important is your ability to use either forecasts or key statistical indicators to predict changes in the direction of the economy and financial markets. Fluctuations in the economy affect the financial markets and an understanding of economic indicators can help you make timely decisions about investments.

4.1   What Is the State of the Economy?

This section explains the effects of the key published economic indicators which can be used to identify trends in the economy. Only the most common indicators will be analyzed.

Gross National Product (GNP) is a measure in dollar value of all the goods and services produced by a country in a year. By comparing

54   Chapter 4

the current GNP with previous years, one can see the economy's rate of growth (or lack of it). Inflation will distort the accuracy of this growth, so there is a measure of the real growth of the nation's output, referred to as "real" GNP. *Real GNP* is adjusted for price level changes and measures each year's goods and services using prices which prevailed in a selected base year. Comparing real GNP figures with those of prior years provides a superior measurement of the real rate of growth. GNP is a measure of the economic health of a country.

Unemployment Rate is the rate of unemployment in a country and is yet another indicator of the economy's strength (or lack of it). The unemployment rate is defined as the percentage of the work force that is out of work. Theoretically, we could define full employment as 100 percent of the work force being employed, but in reality, there are always unemployed people. Therefore, economists and government officials have come to accept a 5-6 percent rate of unemployment as full employment. (Confused? You're not alone.)

When the rate of unemployment rises above the 7 percent level, governments become concerned and will more than likely stimulate the economy (using monetary and fiscal policies) to reduce the unemployment rate. Such actions may have the side effect of increasing inflation.

In 1974 and again in the early 1980s, the U. S. experienced high rates of both unemployment and inflation. The government chose to deal with inflation first, which meant that economic policies were restrictive in trying to reduce the rate of inflation. What followed were recessions, periods of rising unemployment and declining economic activity.

Consumer Price Index (CPI) is a statistic that is calculated monthly by the Bureau of Labor Statistics. Changes in the prices of items (such as food, housing, clothing, transportation, medical care and entertainment) in the CPI are monitored. The CPI measures the rate of inflation and is more meaningful when it is compared relative to previous years. It is, therefore, a gauge of inflation.

Economists feel that the CPI is part of the problem of inflation due to the fact that social security payments and many cost of living increases in employment contracts are tied to changes in the CPI. The CPI may, in fact, overstate the level of inflation.

Economic policy can be quite restrictive when the rates of inflation are higher than policy makers would like.

Producer Price Index (PPI) is a monthly statistic which monitors the costs of the raw materials used to produce products. The PPI is a better indicator of inflation than the CPI, because when raw materials go up in price, there will be a time lag before consumers experience price increases.

How To Read the Financial Pages   55

Price increases and inflation generally will have a detrimental effect on the bond and stock markets as well as on the economy. There is an inverse relationship between inflation and real GNP. When inflation rises, real GNP falls (in 1980 in the U.S.) and the opposite (in 1983 in the U.S) as inflation declines, real GNP rises.

Housing Starts released monthly, represent strength in the rate of housing production. When housing starts increase relative to previous months, more people are buying homes due to optimism about the economy. Thus, strength in housing starts indicates consumer confidence in the economy.

Leading Indicators: Economists have designed an index of leading indicators to forecast economic activity. This index of leading indicators includes data series ranging from stock prices, new building permits and average work week to changes in business and consumer debt. By analyzing this monthly index, economists hope to be able to forecast economic turns, in order to give advance warning of a turn in the stock market. In reality, however, when the leading indicators forecast an economic turn, the stock market has already reacted to the change.

These are some of the ways in which the state of the economy can be monitored. Of course, everyone has an opinion on the economy but by studying the key statistics, that opinion can become more "fine tuned" in order to better anticipate the effects on the market.

4.2 The Effects of the Economy on the Stock Markets

Since publicly held companies make up a large part of the economy, they will be affected by its strengths and weaknesses. Generally, there is a strong correlation between how well companies do — which is tied to their stock prices — and the strength of the economy. When the economy is strong (real GNP is growing, unemployment is falling, raw material orders are increasing, investment spending is up), most firms see sales increases followed by increases in earnings, which allow for increases in dividends and/or growth in the companies. This generally results in higher stock prices.

The relationships of the components of the economy are exceptionally complex and must not be oversimplified. For example, an expanding economy can result in rising prices (inflation), higher wages, increased competition, higher interest rates and higher taxes, all of which could have a detrimental effect on companies' earnings. Thus, the relationship between the economy and the stock market is not a simple one.

56   Chapter 4

It is generally true, however, that during periods of prosperity, stock prices have a tendency to go up.

The opposite is true of a recession where there is a downturn in economic activity and companies eventually feel the effects. Sales slow down and eventually decline leading to reduced earnings and, therefore, lower stock prices.

This points to the overall relationship of economic activity, earnings and stock prices. An expanding economy is generally accompanied by a strong stock market and a declining economy with a weak market. However, we should be wary of blanket generalizations. Not all companies will suffer during periods of economic downturn and, similarly, not all companies will do well during periods of economic growth. Investors will still need to analyze the individual company as to its potential sales and earnings growth and financial position to ascertain whether and when they should purchase that company's stock. By forecasting the direction of the economy, investors can anticipate the direction of the stock market.

4.3   Monetary Policy and the Financial Markets

Monetary policy can have a substantial impact on the economy and thus, the financial markets. The Federal Reserve Bank (Fed) controls the nation's supply of money. By regulating the supply of credit and money, the Fed can affect the country's economic growth, inflation, unemployment and production.

How the Federal Reserve Changes the Supply of Money

The principal tools used by the Federal Reserve Bank to change the supply of money are:

- open market operations;
- reserve requirements; and
- discount rates.

Open Market Operations   The Federal Reserve Bank buys and sells securities in the open market to change the money supply and the reserves of commercial banks. When the Fed buys government securities, it expands the nation's supply of money; it pays for the securities by check which increases the reserves in banks and banks will be able to increase their loans and deposits.

How To Read the Financial Pages   57

When the Fed wants to contract the nation's money supply, it sells government securities from its portfolio on the open market. This has the effect of siphoning off money from the nations money supply causing commercial banks to have reduced reserves and leading to a reduced ability to lend money.

Reserve Requirements   The Federal Reserve Bank requires banks to maintain reserves with the Fed. The percentage of bank deposits that equal reserves is determined by the Fed and is called the *reserve requirements.* The Fed can increase the money supply by reducing the reserve requirements: banks will need to keep less reserves and can therefore increase their lending. The reverse is true when the Fed increases the reserve requirements.

Not only will the money supply increase or decrease due to changes in the reserve requirements, a multiplier effect will also occur. This can be illustrated by using a simple example:

If $100 is deposited in Bank X and the reserve requirements are 10 percent, Bank X now has $100 on deposit of which $10 is kept on reserve and $90 is lent to Corporation A. Corporation A deposits this $90 check in Bank A. Bank A will keep $9 on reserve and lend the remaining $81. This process is repeated, which shows how the original $100 is increased through the banking system to expand the money supply. Figure 4.1 illustrates the multiplier process graphically.

The Fed can stimulate the multiplier effect by lowering the reserve requirements or can reduce the effect on the money supply by raising reserve requirements which will correspondingly increase or decrease the banks' capacities to lend.

Discount Rate   The third available tool, the discount rate, is the rate of interest charged to banks when they borrow from the Fed. When the discount rate is too high, banks are discouraged from borrowing reserves from the Fed. When the discount rate is low or lowered, banks are encouraged to borrow. Thus, using the discount rate, the Fed can expand or contract the money supply.

Defining the Money Supply

Before looking at the relationship of money supply and the financial markets, the different ways of measuring the money supply must be defined. This can be likened to measuring your personal money supply (although a bit finite by comparison!).

Figure 4.1

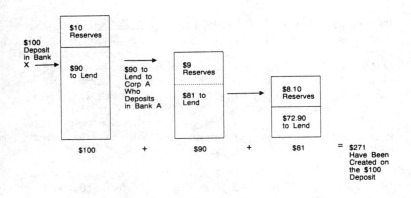

How much cash do you have—the cash in your pockets, wallets, under your mattress and in your checking accounts? Savings accounts, money market funds and some investments can easily be converted into cash. How does this affect the money supply? When categorizing the nations money supply, the measures are referred to as M-1, M-2 and M-3.

M-1 consists of the nation's cash, coins, traveler's checks, checking accounts (NOW accounts which are interest-bearing checking accounts are included) and demand deposits.

M-2 includes M-1 but also adds savings and time deposit accounts (e.g., CDs, money market deposit accounts).

M-3 includes M-1 and M-2 as well as time deposits and financial instruments of large financial institutions.

With these three definitions of the money supply, you can see at once that M-1 could increase when you transfer money from your savings accounts to checking accounts without affecting M-2. There will be discrepancies between the classifications of the money supply from week to week but you should be more concerned with the overall changes over a period of time so that a trend can be established. By monitoring the Fed's open market transactions, changes in the reserve requirements and the discount rate, along with the rate of growth or decline in the money supply, you are better able to make investment decisions.

Impact on the Financial Markets

When the Fed pursues a restrictive monetary policy, it may sell securities on the open market to siphon off money from the money supply and/or raise the reserve requirements which reduces the capacity of banks to lend money and/or raise the discount rate which discourages banks from borrowing money.

These changes in the monetary conditions have an effect on the earnings of companies. When the money supply is decreased, interest rates go up, making it more costly for companies and individuals to borrow money. This causes them to delay their purchases and leads to reduced sales. With lowered sales and higher credit costs, companies have decreased earnings, translating to lower stock prices.

Secondly, when interest rates are on their way up, investors are able to earn more by investing in fixed income securities and money market instruments. Therefore, many investors take their money out of the stock markets and invest in liquid short-term securities and longer term debt securities, putting more downward pressure on stock prices. Thirdly, higher interest rates translate into higher borrowing costs for margin investors. These investors move their money to debt instruments to justify their higher interest costs.

Monetary policy has a direct effect on interest rates and there is a strong correlation between interest rates and the stock market. Rising interest rates tend to depress stock market prices and falling interest rates have the opposite effect.

The open market operations of the Fed have a direct impact on interest rates and the bond markets. When the Fed buys Treasury securities on the open market it competes with other buyers, driving up prices and causing a decrease in their yields. This creates a rate discrepancy between the yields on government debt and corporate debt. As a result, investors will purchase corporate debt which will cause their prices to go up and their yields to decrease. The reverse is true when the Fed sells government securities on the open market.

60   Chapter 4

This suggests that if investors anticipate changes in monetary policy, they can make the appropriate changes to their investment strategies.

4.4   Fiscal Policy and the Markets

The goals of monetary and fiscal policy are the same: the pursuit of full employment, economic growth and price stability. The government can stimulate or restrain the economy in its pursuit of economic goals through its fiscal policy. The tools of fiscal policy are taxation, government expenditure and the government's debt management. Changes in fiscal policy can affect the financial markets.

Taxation

Taxation is used by the federal government to raise revenue and also to reduce the amount of money in the economy. Taxation policies can stimulate or depress the economy and the stock markets. When there are large tax increases, consumers as a whole have less money to invest and spend on goods and services; and corporations have reduced earnings leading to lower dividends.

Tax cuts, however, have the opposite effect. Individuals have more money to spend and invest and corporations experience the benefits of greater consumer spending and lower corporate taxes which generally lead to higher sales and higher earnings.

Government Spending

The effect of a tax cut is similar to that of an increase in government spending. A tax cut has a favorable effect on savings and investments whereas government spending has a greater effect on the goods and services produced in the economy. Government spending can also be used as a tool to stimulate or restrain the economy.

Debt Management

When its revenues are less than its expenditures, the government runs a deficit. Deficit spending can have a significant effect on the financial markets in general and the stock market in particular. The government can finance its deficit by:

- borrowing in the financial markets, or

How To Read the Financial Pages   61

- increasing the money supply.

By borrowing in the financial markets, the government drives up yields on the bond markets which has a depressing effect on the stock market. By selling securities on the market, prices of government securities go down which increases their yields. To counter the rate differential (between corporate and government securities), investors invest in government securities rather than in corporate securities, thereby reducing the prices of corporate bonds leading to increased yields (on corporate bonds). Thus, borrowing in the market by the government has the effect of depressing bond prices and increasing interest rates. The opposite is true of the government buying securities in the market: bond prices are pushed up and interest rates are lowered.

When a government is faced with having to finance an increasing deficit from year to year, it will have to pay high rates of interest to attract buyers to invest in all its securities. This leads to higher interest rates in the economy which, as discussed, has a depressing effect on stock prices.

If the government increases the money supply, it may cause inflation to raise its "ugly head"; inflation does not have a wonderful effect on the economy or the stock market.

In summary, when a government is unable to reduce the growth of its deficit spending, there is a depressing effect on the stock market. Investors constantly look for policies or budgets that can effectively change the direction of the deficit's growth which would then have a beneficial effect on the stock market. Fiscal policies affect the security markets and by anticipating changes in the policies, you can formulate your investment strategies.

4.5   The Stock Markets and How To Read Stock Prices

The stock markets — where you can buy and sell your shares of stock — and news about different stocks seem to take up a major portion of the financial pages. Stocks may be listed on the New York Stock Exchange, American Stock Exchange, and/or regional exchanges. If stocks are not listed on these exchanges, they may be traded on the over-the-counter markets.

Exchanges

The New York Stock Exchange (NYSE) is the largest and oldest exchange in the U.S. and has the most stringent listing requirements. Generally,

62   Chapter 4

the largest, best known, financially secure companies are listed on the NYSE.

The American Stock Exchange (AMEX) has less stringent listing requirements than the NYSE and generally has the listings of younger, smaller companies.

Regional Exchanges: There are fourteen regional exchanges which list the stocks of companies in their geographic areas. A company can be listed on the NYSE or AMEX and also be listed on a regional exchange.

Over-the-Counter Market (OTC): A number of companies that issue stock to the public may not be listed on any of the exchanges for a variety of reasons. Instead they are traded over-the-counter, a marketplace linked by a network of computers and telephones.

The most actively traded issues are listed on the NASDAQ (National Association of Securities Dealers Automated Quotations) national market system and the less heavily traded issues are listed on the NASDAQ bid and ask quotations. The least actively traded issues are listed on the Additional Over-the-Counter Quotes. A stockbroker can, therefore, provide the bid and asked price for a particular stock by punching that company's code into the NASDAQ computer system. There are many large reputable companies, (Apple Computer and MCI for example) that have chosen to remain on the OTC market rather than move up to AMEX or NYSE.

Stock Market Indices

Stock investors are always anxious to know how the stock market is doing, whether the market is going up or down and, of course, when to buy and sell stocks. This results in a variety of stock market measures and analyses. The question many investors ask is:

"Why should we be so concerned with these aggregate measures of the stock market?"

The obvious answer is that those aggregate measures will have a direct effect on individual stocks in the market. However, before becoming panic stricken and ordering your broker to sell your stocks when you read that the Dow Jones Industrial Average has dropped forty points in one day; or becoming jubilant and ordering champagne for the neighborhood when the Standard & Poor's 500 Index goes up, you should first see how these indices relate to the overall composition of your stock portfolio before taking any action.

Individual measures of the market are indicators or gauges of the stock market which are convenient to use. By using these measures, it is possible to compare how well your individual stocks performed against a comparable market indicator for the same period.

There are two measures of stock market prices: an average and an index. An average is calculated by adding stock prices and then dividing by a number to give the average price. The Dow Jones Averages are computed this way. An *index* is a more sophisticated weighting of stock prices which are related to a base year's stock prices. Examples are the Standard & Poor's 500 Composite Index, NYSE Composite Index and the OTC Index.

Dow Jones Industrial Average (DJIA) is the oldest and most widely quoted average. The DJIA is composed of the stock prices of thirty large, blue-chip companies (see Table 4.1) which are listed on the NYSE. Stock prices are added and then divided by an adjusted divisor. This divisor is a very small number (.559 in 1991) making the DJIA a greater number than the average of the stock prices.

There is also the Dow Jones Transportation Average (DJTA) which is composed of the stocks of the twenty major transportation companies; the Dow Jones Utility Average (DJUA) which includes fifteen major utility stocks; and the Dow Jones Composite Average which combines the three Dow Jones Indices and consists of all the stocks of the sixty-five companies. See Table 4.1 for a listing of the companies.

Much criticism surrounds the DJIA. First, the stocks are not equally weighted so that an increase of a higher priced stock will have a greater impact on the DJIA than an increase of a lower priced stock. Secondly, with a sample of only thirty large stocks, the DJIA is hardly a representative measure of the market.

The DJIA can, however, be of use to you. First, by looking at a chart of the DJIA over a period of time, you can see the ups and downs of the market which will assist in deciding when to buy and sell stocks. Secondly, the DJIA can be used as a yardstick for comparing how your stocks have performed in comparison to the DJIA for the same period of time. However, since the DJIA is composed of only thirty stocks (approximately 25 percent of the total market value of all the stocks traded on the NYSE), you can look at more broad-based measures of the market.

Standard & Poor's Index (S & P 500) consists of 500 stocks listed on the NYSE. The 500 companies in the S & P 500 Index can also be monitored as follows: the S & P Industrial Index which consists of 400 industrial stocks; the S & P Transportation Index of twenty companies; the S & P Utilities Index of forty companies and the S & P Financial Index of forty companies.

The S & P 500 Index is a market value weighted index which is computed by calculating the total market value of the 500 companies in

64   Chapter 4

Table 4.1

Dow Jones Industrial Average

Allied Signal	Eastman Kodak	J.P. Morgan & Co.
Alcoa	Exxon Corp.	Philip Morris Co.
American Express	General Electric	Procter & Gamble
A T & T	General Motors	Sears, Roebuck
Bethlehem Steel	Goodyear Tire	Texaco Inc.
Boeing	IBM	Union Carbide
Caterpillar Inc.	International Paper	United Technologies
Chevron	McDonalds Corp.	Walt Disney Co.
Coca-Cola	Merck & Co.	Westinghouse Electric
Du Pont	Minnesota Mining & Mfg.	Woolworth

Dow Jones Transportation Average

AMR Corp.	Consolidated Freight	Santa Fe Southern Pacific
Airborn Freight	Conrail	Southwest Air
Alaska Air	Delta Airlines	UAL Corp.
American President Lines	Federal Express	Union Pacific Corp.
Burlington Northern	Norfolk & Southern	U.S. Air
CSX Corp.	Roadway Services*	XTRA Corp.
Carolina Freight	Ryder System	

Dow Jones Utility Average

American Electric Power	Consolidated Natural Gas	Panhandle Eastern Corp.
Arkla	Detroit Edison	Peoples Energy
Centerior Energy	Houston Industries	Philadelphia Electric
Commonwealth Edison	Niagara Mohawk Power	Public Service Enterprises
Consolidated Edison	Pacific Gas & Electric	So. Cal. Edison Corp.

* NASDAQ National Market System

---

the index and comparing the total market value of the 500 companies the previous day. The percentage of increase or decrease in the total market value from one day to the next represents the change in the index.

Approximately 75 percent of the total market value of all the companies listed on the NYSE are represented in the S&P 500 Index, making it an even broader-based gauge of market activity than the DJIA.

New York Stock Exchange Composite Index is a more broad-based measure than the S & P Index because it includes all the stocks traded on the NYSE. It is a market value weighted index and like the S & P 500, relates to a base period which is December 31, 1965. On that date, the NYSE Composite Index was fifty. In addition to the NYSE Composite Index, the NYSE also has indices for industrials, utilities, transportation and financial stocks.

NASDAQ Composite Index is a measure of all the stocks traded on the NASDAQ (National Association of Securities Dealers Automated Quotations) system. The NASDAQ Index shows more volatility than the DJIA and the S & P 500 Index, because the companies traded on the over-the-counter market are smaller and more speculative. An increase in the NASDAQ Composite Index can be interpreted as investor enthusiasm for small stocks.

Other Indices

The American Stock Exchange (AMEX) Index is value weighted and includes all the stocks listed on that exchange.

Wilshire 5000 is the broadest index and includes all the companies listed on the NYSE and AMEX, as well as many of the larger stocks traded on the over-the-counter market.

Value Line Composite Index differs from the other indices in that it is calculated using a geometric averaging technique of 1700 stocks listed on the NYSE, AMEX and the OTC markets.

The obvious question is which is the best index to use? Unfortunately, there is no obvious answer. Studies have shown that all the indices are correlated — they all move together in the same direction, but there will be some differences. The NASDAQ and AMEX indices are not as highly correlated with S & P 500 and DJIA — the stocks of the former two indices are composed of companies which are younger, smaller and riskier than the stocks of the larger companies of the DJIA and S & P 500 Index.

Choose the index that closely resembles the make-up of your stock portfolios so that you can evaluate the performance of your stocks against the index.

How To Read Common Stock Quotations

The format for reading stock price quotations is the same for stocks listed on the NYSE, AMEX and NASDAQ National Market System.

The market prices of listed stocks are quoted daily in the financial pages of the newspapers. For example, the stock of Alleghany which is traded on the NYSE is shown in Figure 4.2.

Investor's Business Daily financial tables include additional information not found in most of the other financial newspapers, such as the earnings per share (EPS) rank and the relative strength. The earnings

66   Chapter 4

Figure 4.2

EPS Rel. Rnk Str.	52-Week High Low	Stock Name	Closing Price	Vol.% Chg. Change	Vol. % 100s Yld.	Day's Price High Low
81 70	90¼ 74½	Alleghany	85¾ + 1⅜ + 109		46 2.0	85¾ 84⅞ k
40 70	34¼ 18⅛	Allegheny Ldl	25½ + 1 + 999		3725 3.5	26 24½
59 56	41 34	Alleghny Pwr	37⅛ + ⅛ − 6		771 8.5	37⅜ 36⅞
93 76	20 9¾	Allen Group	13½ + ⅛ − 48		92	13½ 13⅛ k
56 93	21¼ 12½	Allergan Inc	21⅛ + ½ + 72		4183 1.5	21⅛ 20 o

Source: *Investor's Business Daily*. Reprinted by permission of *Investor's Business Daily*, *America's Business Newspaper*, (February 1, 1991), © *Investor's Business Daily, Inc.* 1991.

per share rank in the first column shows the relative stability and growth of the company's earnings per share. The rankings are from one to ninety-nine. Alleghany's rank of eighty-one indicates that it has achieved earnings in the top 19 percent of all the companies in the tables. The second column shows the company's relative price strength relative to other stocks. Stocks are ranked between one and ninety-nine. Stocks with rankings below seventy indicate weaker price performance. Over the past fifty-two weeks, Alleghany stock reached its high of $90.25 per share and its low of $74.50 per share. The fifth column shows the name of the stock. The closing price is the last price of the day. The change column indicates that Alleghany went up 1 3/8 of a point from the previous day's closing price. The volume % change column shows whether the trading volume is above or below its average daily volume. Alleghany traded 109 percent more than its normal volume on that day. The next column shows the total shares traded for Alleghany to be 4600. When following the progress of a particular stock, you can assume when the volume of the stock is greater than the normal range of daily trading that there is some development of consequence. The dividend yield is 2 percent which can be found by dividing the dividend by the closing price. For this stock, the dividend is $1.715 per share (1.715/85.75). The next two columns indicate the day's high and low price.

Some financial newspapers indicate the stock's price to earnings (P/E) ratio. The P/E ratio indicates what price investors are willing to pay in relation to a company's earnings. (The P/E ratio is the stock price divided by the earnings per share). Growth stocks tend to have high P/E multiples whereas blue-chips are characterized by low P/E ratios.

Bid and Asked Quotations

Over-the-counter stocks which are not quoted on the National Market issues are quoted on a bid and asked basis. For example, the stock of ACTV is traded on the NASDAQ Bid and Asked Quotations and is shown in Figure 4.3.

ACTV pays no dividend as there are no figures indicated after the name. The bid price indicates that buyers of ACTV stock were willing to pay $2.375 per share, and the asked price indicates that sellers were willing to sell at $2.625 per share. The net change shows that the stock price closed 1/8 of a point higher than the previous day's closing price.

Preferred Stock Quotations

Preferred stock, a hybrid of debt and common stock, is listed with the common stocks on the stock exchanges. Preferred stock pays dividends at a rate which is fixed at the time of its issue. Although the payments of preferred dividends are not legal obligations of companies, companies cannot pay dividends to common stockholders before they have paid their preferred stockholders. Bearing in mind these differences, preferred stock is read the same way as common stock in the stock exchange quotations.

Figure 4.3

Stock	Bid	Ask	Chg
- A-B -			
ACS Enterprs	1¼	1 $\frac{7}{16}$ +	$\frac{7}{16}$
A C T V Inc	2⅜	2⅝ +	⅛
ACTV wt	1¼	1½	....
ADM Tronics	⅜	$\frac{13}{32}$ +	$\frac{3}{32}$

Source: *Investor's Business Daily.* Reprinted by permission of *Investor's Business Daily, America's Business Newspaper,* (February 1, 1991), © *Investor's Business Daily, Inc.* 1991.

68   Chapter 4

4.6 The Bond Markets and How To Read Bond Prices

Bonds are issued by corporations, the federal government, agencies of the federal government, municipal governments, foreign corporations and governments.

Exchanges

A number of corporate bonds are listed on the New York Bond Exchange and the American Bond Exchange. Bonds are also traded over-the-counter among bond dealers.

There is an active secondary market for Treasury securities and corporate bonds.

There is also a secondary market for government agency bonds such as FNMAs, GNMAs and municipal bonds such as state and local government issues, highway authorities and foreign bonds.

Indices

Bond market indices differ from equity market indices in two respects. Bond market indices are not followed as extensively as stock market indices in order to gauge how well the market is doing, and they focus on rates of return or bond prices whereas equity indices focus on price movements only. There are several indices for assessing the behavior of the bond markets.

The *Dow Jones Bond Average* consists of ten utility bonds and ten industrial bonds. The focus is on the closing prices of these bonds and the average shows the percentage of face value that these bonds would sell at (Figure 4.4).

Shearson Lehman Hutton Indices These indices are more extensive than the Dow Jones Bond Average.

The *Corporate Bond Index* includes all the publicly issued debt of industrial, finance, and utility companies whose issues are non-convertible and have a fixed rate. Only bonds with maturities of at least one year or more and a minimum outstanding principal balance of $25 million are included.

The *Government Bond Index* includes all the publicly issued debt of the federal government and its agencies whose issues are non-convertible and have fixed rates. Only issues with a maturity of one year or more and a principal balance of $25 million are included.

Figure 4.4

For Thursday, January 31, 1991

Dow Jones Bond Averages

	— 1989 —		Today's	Change
	High	Low	Close	Points
20 Bonds	94.15	87.35	92.84	− 0.01
Utilities	95.26	86.95	94.54	− 0.15
Indust.	93.26	87.60	91.15	+ 0.14
Commod			124.93	− 0.23

Source: *Investor's Business Daily*. Reprinted by permission of *Investor's Business Daily, America's Business Newspaper*, (February 1, 1991), © *Investor's Business Daily, Inc.* 1991.

The Treasury Bond Index includes debt issues of the U.S. Treasury.

The Mortgage-Backed Securities Index includes all the fixed rate debt issues which are backed by the mortgages of the GNMA, FNMA and the Federal Home Loan Corporation.

The Yankee Bond Index includes U.S. dollar bonds registered with the SEC which are issued or backed by non-U.S. governments.

The Government Corporate Bond Index combines the Government Bond Index and the Corporate Bond Index. It is the most representative of the bond market indices.

Barron's Confidence Index This index is the ratio of Barron's average yield of ten high grade corporate bonds to the yield on the more speculative Dow Jones average of forty bonds. It shows the yield spread between high grade bonds and more speculative bonds.

Users of the index believe that during periods of optimism investors will invest more in speculative bonds (to get the higher rate of return), which will push their prices up and lower their yields. This causes the confidence index to increase.

Other notable bond indices include the Salomon Brothers Indices, Bond Buyer Municipal Index and the Merrill Lynch Corporate Index.

Although bond market indices are not as widely known or used as the stock market indicators, they are becoming more important. More investors have been investing in bonds and fixed income mutual funds

70   Chapter 4

during the 1980s and these indices are excellent yardsticks for investors to evaluate the performance of their fixed income investments.

How To Read Bond Quotations

Corporate Bonds: Daily quotations of bonds listed on the New York and American Exchanges can be found in financial newspapers, such as *Investor's Business Daily*. Figure 4.5 from *Investor's Business Daily*, February 1, 1991, shows the listings of several corporate bonds.

The first column shows the S & P rating for each of the listed bonds with AAA indicating bonds of the highest quality, followed by AA and then A down to the lowest rating — D — representing bonds in default. Alcoa bonds have an A rating which indicates that the principal and interest repayments are considered to be secure but could be impaired in the future. Following the name of the bond is the exchange listing. Alcoa and all the other bonds in this example are listed on the New York Exchange. Other bond exchanges are the American, Over-the-Counter and the Pacific. The coupon rate for Alcoa is 7.45 percent (i.e., each bondholder will receive $74.50 in interest per year until November 1996 when the bonds mature). The figures following the coupon rate indicate the date of maturity — November 1996.

The current yield, 7.9 percent, is determined by dividing the interest received ($74.50 the coupon rate) by the market price ($940) at the close of the day, (74.50/940 = 7.9 percent). The yield to maturity includes current income from the bond as well as the repayment of the par value of the bond at maturity. If the Alcoa bond is purchased at $940 and held

---

Figure 4.5

S&P Rat- ing	Bond	Ex	Cou- pon Rate	Mat- ures	Cur. Yld.	Yld. to Mat.	Vol.	Bond Close	Chg
AA	AlaskaHsg	NY	10.750	06/93	10.5	9.8	9	102	...
A	AlbmaPwr	NY	10.875	10/05	10.4	10.2	11	105	+ 1½
A	AlbmaPwr	NY	8.875	08/03	9.0	9.1	4	98⅝	...
A	AlbmaPwr	NY	9.625	03/08	9.5	9.5	10	100⅞	− ⅛
A	AlbmaPwr	NY	9.500	02/08	9.5	9.5	10	100	− ⅛
A	AlbmaPwr	NY	10.500	12/05	10.0	9.8	15	105⅜	+ ⅜
A	AlbmaPwr	NY	9.750	08/04	9.6	9.5	18	101¾	• ...
A	Alcoa	NY	7.450	11/96	7.9	8.8	10	94	− ½
A	AldCorp	NY	ZrCpn	01/96	...	9.4	132	63½	+ 1⅜
A	AldCorp	NY	ZrCpn	08/01	...	10.0	10	36	+ 1⅜

Source: *Investor's Business Daily*. Reprinted by permission of *Investor's Business Daily, America's Business Newspaper*, (February 1, 1991), © *Investor's Business Daily, Inc.* 1991.

to maturity, the purchaser would receive a return of 8.8 percent. The volume is quoted in dollar terms: $10,000 of Alcoa bonds were traded on that particular day. Bonds are quoted in 100s (the last digit is dropped—a $1,000 face value bond is quoted as $100). Bonds under 100 are selling at a discount and over 100 are selling at a premium. The closing price for Alcoa is $940. The net change column shows the change from the previous day's close; in this case Alcoa was down by 1/2 point.

Corporate Convertible Bonds are listed on the same exchanges and read the same way as corporate bonds.

A *cy* in the current yield column would signify that it is a convertible bond.

Zero-Coupon Bonds are quoted in the same tables as corporate bonds. A *zr* following the name of the bond would signify that it is a zero-coupon bond. There would be no coupon rate as zero-coupon bonds pay no periodic interest.

Municipal Bonds: The following quote for Atlanta Georgia Revenue Bonds as quoted in the Tax Exempt Bonds listed in *Investor's Business Daily*, February 1, 1991, reads as follows in Figure 4.6.

The first column shows both the Moody's and Standard and Poor's ratings. For the tax-exempt *issue* Atlanta Georgia Airport Facilities Revenue Service Bonds, backed by the revenues raised by the project which was financed by these bonds, the Moody and S & P ratings are A. Following the name is the *coupon rate*, which is the percentage of par value that is paid in interest. These bonds pay 7.25 percent of par ($1,000) which is $72.50 in interest per bond per year. The *maturity* date is the date that the bonds will be retired (paid back)—January 1, 2017.

Figure 4.6

	TRANSPORTATION						
A/A	ATLANTA GA AIRPORT FACILITIES REVENUE SER	7¼	01/01/17	98⅞	+	⅛	7.35
A3/A	ATLANTA GA REVENUE SER 89B AMT DELTA AIR L	7⅞	12/01/18	101	+	⅛	7.81
A3/A–	CHICAGO O'HARE SPEC FAC REV (AMERICAN) 90A	7⅞	11/01/25	96⅝		..	8.17
A3/A–	DALLAS–FT WORTH INTL AIRPORT AMERICAN AIR	8	11/01/24	96½	+	⅛	8.31
A/A	KENTUCKY TURNPIKE AUTH ECON DEV ROAD REVEN	7¼	05/15/10	100⅝	+	⅛	7.19
Aaa/AAA	ORLANDO–ORANGE CO EXPRESSWAY AUTH FLA JR L	6¾	07/01/19	97⅝		..	6.95
Aaa/AAA	SAN MATEO CO TRANSIT DIST CALIF SERIES 90A	6½	06/01/20	95⅜	+	⅜	6.87
Aa/AA+	TRIBOROUGH BRIDGE & TUNNEL AUTH NY REVENUE	7	01/01/21	98¼	+	⅛	7.14

Source: *Investor's Business Daily*. Reprinted by permission of *Investor's Business Daily, America's Business Newspaper*, (February 1, 1991), © *Investor's Business Daily, Inc.* 1991.

The next column is the dollar *bid price* of the bonds which is $98.875 ($988.75 per bond). The *change* indicates the difference from the previous day's bid price. In this case, the bonds increased 1/8th of a percentage point from the previous day's bid price. The last column is the yield to maturity. If investors bought these bonds, paid $988.75 per bond and held them until January 1, 2017, their return would be 7.35 percent.

A separate table lists *Treasury Bonds and Notes* in the financial newspapers. The issues are listed in order of maturity. The following listings (Figure 4.7) are taken from the Table of Government Bonds and Notes as quoted from *Investor's Business Daily* February 1, 1991.

The Coupon Rate in the first column signifies the percentage of par value that is paid as interest. The Treasury note indicated by the arrows pays interest of $85 per year. The *s* indicates that the interest payments are made semi-annually ($42.50 every six months).

The Maturity Date is when the note matures – May 1991. A *p* after the date signifies that it is a Treasury note for which non-resident aliens are exempt from withholding tax. An *n* indicates that it is a regular Treasury note. Treasury bonds and notes are quoted on a *bid and asked* basis. The *bid* price is the highest price offered by buyers of this issue: they are willing to pay 100 13/32 or $1,004.06 per note. The *asked* price is the lowest price offered by sellers: sellers are asking 100 17/32 or $1,005.31 per note. The *change* shows the change in 32nds of a point between the bid price as quoted here and the bid price as quoted the previous day. For this issue, there is no change from the previous day's bid price. The *yield* is the return investors would get if they paid the

Figure 4.7

GOVT. BONDS & NOTES

7⅜s	2-91 p	99.31	100.3	+ .1	4.74
9⅛s	2-91 p	100.2	100.6	+ .1	4.02
9⅜s	2-91 p	100.5	100.9	..	5.37
6¾s	3-91 p	99.31	100.3	..	6.02
9¾s	3-91 p	100.14	100.18	+ .1	5.99
12⅜s	4-91 n	101.3	101.7	+ .1	6.00
9¼s	4-91 p	100.20	100.24	+ .1	5.98
→ 8⅛s	5-91 p	100.13	100.17	..	6.12 ←
14½s	5-91 n	102.5	102.9	..	6.15
8¾s	5-91 p	100.22	100.26	..	6.12
7⅞s	6-91 n	100.15	100.19	..	6.35
8¼s	6-91 p	100.20	100.24	..	6.33
7¾s	7-91 p	100.17	100.21	..	6.39
13¾s	7-91 n	103.4	103.8	+ .1	6.33
7½s	8-91 p	100.14	100.18	..	6.41

Source: *Investor's Business Daily*. Reprinted by permission of *Investor's Business Daily, America's Business Newspaper*, (February 1, 1991), © *Investor's Business Daily, Inc.* 1991.

asked price for the note and held it until maturity. The return is 6.12 percent.

Government Agency Bonds are listed and read the same as Treasury notes and bonds.

Treasury Bills are quoted separately in a section marked *Treasury bills* in most financial newspapers and listed in order of their maturity. The following (Figure 4.8) Treasury bill quote is from *Investor's Business Daily*, February 1, 1991.

Treasury bills are short-term securities, so all the listed T-bills will *mature* within one year. The issue marked by arrows matured on March 14, 1991. Treasury bills are sold at a discount which is less than the par or face amount of $1,000 and then redeemed at par at maturity. This difference is attributed to interest. The *bid* discount of 6.1 percent was the highest discount (price) that a dealer was willing to buy on that day, and the *asked* discount of 6.06 percent was the lowest discount that a dealer was willing to sell on that day.

The dealer's selling price can be calculated as follows:

$$= \quad \$100 - 100 \ (0.0606) \ 42^* \ / \ 360$$
$$= \quad \underline{\$99.293 \ or \ \$992.93 \ per \ T\text{-bill}}$$

The dealer's purchase price:

$$= \quad 100 - 100 \ (0.0610) \ 42^* \ / \ 360$$
$$= \quad \underline{\$99.2883 \ or \ \$992.88 \ per \ T\text{-bill}}$$

* the number of days to settlement from February 1, 1991.

Figure 4.8

T-BILLS

Mat. Date	Bid	Asked	Bid Chg.	Yield
1-17 91	5.21	5.00	..	5.07
2-07 91	5.16	5.03 −	.50	5.11
2-14 91	5.39	5.31 −	.45	5.40
2-21 91	5.57	5.53	..	5.63
2-28 91	5.30	5.28 −	.07	5.38
3-07 91	5.82	5.78 − ·	.05	5.89
3-14 91	6.10	6.06 +	.01	6.19
3-21 91	6.09	6.06 +	.01	6.20
3-28 91	6.06	6.03 +	.03	6.17

Source: *Investor's Business Daily*. Reprinted by permission of *Investor's Business Daily*, *America's Business Newspaper*, (February 1, 1991), © *Investor's Business Daily, Inc.* 1991.

74   Chapter 4

The *ask yield* is 6.19 percent which is the return an investor would get on this issue if bought at the asked discount.

4.7 How To Read Mutual Fund Quotations

Mutual fund quotations are listed in the daily newspapers as well as in the financial newspapers. See Figure 4.9 for an excerpt of Mutual Funds from *Investor's Business Daily*, February 1, 1991.

The investment companies that sell shares in these funds are listed alphabetically and then the respective funds in each of the investment companies are listed. For example, the Vanguard Group offers a variety of different funds beginning with the Asset Allocation fund, followed by the Bond Market Fund. The *NAV* stands for net asset value which is the amount an investor would pay to buy a share if that fund is a no load fund. In the Vanguard Group, for example, all the funds are no load indicated by the *NL*. This means that the net asset value is the same as the offer price so an investor would pay $11.70 to buy a share in the Asset Allocation Fund. Similarly, if the investor wanted to sell shares back to Vanguard on this day, Vanguard would buy them back at $11.70 per share. The column *NAVchange* indicates that for the Asset Allocation Fund, the NAV increased by $.07 from the previous day's net asset value.

Investor's Business Daily includes their performance rankings of the mutual funds in the first column. The rankings of the mutual funds are based on their total return which includes dividends and capital gains. The top 5 percent of mutual funds have an A+ rating, the top 10 percent have an A rating, the top 15 percent an A–, the top 20 percent a B+, the top 25 percent a B, the top 30 percent a B–, the top 35 percent a C+, the top 40 percent a C, top 45 percent a C–, the top 50 percent a D+ and so on, to all those mutual funds below 70 percent which would get an E rating. The year-to-date total percentage change gives the total change in return for the year. Thus, the Vanguard Bond Market fund has a C– rating which indicates that in terms of total return for the year period, it ranked in the top 45 percent of all the mutual funds. For the year to date it increased its return by 1 percent. The next column shows the type of fund: *g* is a growth fund, *i* is an income fund, *o* is a bond fund, *y* is a balanced fund, *w* is an international fund and *s* is a specialized fund.

By looking at the Van Kampen Merritt group, in Figure 4.9, you will see that all their funds are load funds. In other words, the net asset values differ from the offer prices. These differences are the commissions which are charged for buying and selling the shares. For example, in the Van Kampen Merritt Funds, the following is the listing for the High Yield Fund.

How To Read the Financial Pages

Figure 4.9

— V — W — X —

Rank	Name	%Chg	Type	Net Asset Value	Offer Price	N.A.V. Chg
E	*Valley Forge*	+ 2	g	8.66	NL+	.01
	Value Line Fund	Assets 1.3 billion				
E	Aggress Income	+ 1	i	6.27	NL+	.02
E	Convertible	+ 3	i	10.38	NL	
A –	Value Line Fund	+ 7	g	15.36	NL+	.09
B+	Income	+ 3	i	6.58	NL+	.04
B+	Leverage Growth	+ 8	g	22.74	NL+	.18
E	TxEx High Yield	+ 1	o	10.24	NL+	.02
	NY Tax Exempt	+ 1	o	9.53	NL+	.02
E	Special Situation	+ 8	g	13.71	NL+	.13
C+	US Govt Secs	+ 1	o	12.12	NL+	.02
	Van Eck	Assets 1.0 billion				
E	Gold Resources p	– 11	s	3.46	3.71+	.01
E	Intl Investors	– 12	w	9.96	10.89+	.01
A –	World Income p	+ 6	w	10.03	10.53+	.04
E	World Trend p	+ 4	w	13.78	14.62+	.09
	Van Kampen Merritt	Assets 5.0 billion				
D+	CA Insured TxFr p	0	o	15.71	16.52+	.01
D	Grwth & Incme p	+ 5	g	16.20	17.03+	.19
E	High Yield p	– 1	o	8.11	8.53	
C –	Insured Tax Free p	+ 1	o	17.93	18.85+	.03
	Municpal Income	0	o	14.31	15.05+	.02
	PA Tax Free	+ 1	o	15.80	16.61+	.02
	Shrt Trn Glb Inc	0	w	9.59	9.89	
D –	TaxFree High Inc p	0	o	15.60	16.40+	.01
C+	US Government p	+ 1	o	15.33	16.12+	.01
	Vance Exchange	Assets 544 million				
B	CapitalExchange	+ 6	g	125.86	NL+1.53	
B+	Depositors Bostn	+ 6	g	66.25	NL+	.41
C+	Diversification	+ 6	i	130.69	NL+	.67
A	Exchange	+ 5	g	189.49	NL+1.60	
D	Exchange Boston	+ 4	g	155.79	NL+	.92
A	Fiduciary Exchng	+ 8	g	112.79	NL+1.09	
B –	Second Fiduciary	+ 6	i	100.74	NL+1.17	
	Vanguard Group	Assets 31 billion				
	Asset Allocation	+ 3	g	11.70	NL+	.07
C –	Bond Market	+ 1	o	9.45	NL+	.01
E	Convertible Secs	+ 6	i	8.68	NL+	.03
	Equity Income	+ 5	i	11.01	NL+	.09
E	Explorer	+ 10	g	28.01	NL+	.40
A	Morgan Growth	+ 6	g	11.02	NL+	.10

1988-1990 Mutual Fund Performance Rank	1991 Total %Chg	Type Of Fund	Net Asset Value	Offer Price Chg N.A.V.

D – MN Tax Free

Weiss Peck Greer — Assets 426 million

Rank	Name	%Chg	Type	Net Asset Value	Offer Price	N.A.V. Chg
C	Tudor	+ 9	g	19.53	NL+	.23
E	WPG	+ 7	g	19.79	NL+	.20
E	Govt Securities	+ 1	o	10.28	NL+	.01
E	Growth	+ 10	g	104.89	NL+1.31	
E	*Wall Street*	+ 12	g	6.17	6.53+	.13
	Wells FargoIRA – 401K	Assets 406 million				
	Asset Allocation	+ 2	g	14.82	NL+	.05
	Corporate Stock	+ 4	g	24.59	NL+	.22
	Fixed Income	+ 1	i	13.26	NL+	.01
	IRA Small Co f	+ 8	g	10.83	NL+	.16
	Westcore	Assets 406 million				
	Short Term Bond	+ 1	o	9.82	10.02	
	Intrmediate Bond	0	o	9.36	9.80	
	Bond Plus	+ 1	o	15.43	16.16+	.02
	Basic Value	+ 6	g	17.63	18.46+	.18
	Modern Value	+ 4	g	11.05	11.57+	.14
	MIDCO Growth	+ 10	g	11.26	11.79+	.13
	Shrt Inter TaxEx	+ 1	o	15.10	15.41	
B –	*Westwood*	+ 6	g	13.29	13.84+	.09
	WlmBlrResInc	....	i	10.20	10.20+	.01
	Wood Struthers	Assets 115 million				
B	Neuwirth	+ 3	g	10.51	NL+	.09
B+	Pine Street	+ 4	g	11.33	NL+	.08
C+	Winthrop Growth t	+ 4	g	10.00	10.00+	.13
	Wright Funds	Assets 587 million				
	Govt Obligation	0	o	12.14	NL+	.03
	Jr Blue Chip	+ 8	g	12.37	NL+	.20
	Near Term Bond	0	o	10.28	NL	
	Quality Core	+ 6	g	11.44	NL+	.12
	Select Blue Chip	+ 4	g	14.40	NL+	.16
	Total Return	0	o	11.76	NL+	.01

— Y — Z —

Rank	Name	%Chg	Type	Net Asset Value	Offer Price	N.A.V. Chg
	Yamaichi Globl	+ 3	w	7.77	8.16+	.06
	Zweig Funds	Assets 489 million				
D –	Govt Securities p	+ 1	o	9.62	10.10+	.01
A –	Strategy	+ 4	g	11.10	11.75+	.09
A –	Priority Select p	+ 4	g	10.67	11.29+	.09
E	Tax Free Ltd Trm	0	o	10.30	10.46	
E	Tax Fr Long Trm p	0	o	9.37	9.79	

1988-1990 Mutual Fund Performance Rank	1991 Total %Chg	Type Of Fund	Net Asset Value	Offer Price Chg N.A.V.

Source: *Investor's Business Daily.* Reprinted by permission of *Investor's Business Daily, America's Business Newspaper,* (February 1, 1991), © *Investor's Business Daily, Inc.* 1991.

The High Yield Fund has a net asset value of $8.11 per share and an offer price of $8.53. If you invested in the High Yield Fund, you would pay $8.53 for a share having a net asset value of $8.11. The $0.42 difference is the commission charged by this fund.

76   Chapter 4

The aim of this chapter has been to explain and simplify some of the everyday economic and financial jargon found in the financial pages of the newspapers. It is not meant to be a comprehensive guide to the understanding of economics and finance. Rather, the objective of this chapter is to help you understand some of the theories affecting the financial markets and to enable you to follow the progress of your investments in the newspapers.

CHAPTER 5

HOW WELL ARE MY INVESTMENTS DOING?

Do you need to be a professional investor to monitor your investments? The answer is obviously "no." It is important to evaluate your investments from time to time to see how well they are doing. Your needs and circumstances change, financial markets go up and down and individual financial assets may no longer be suitable. Regardless of the techniques you use to evaluate your investments, you need to establish a norm to see which investments are superior and which are substandard.

You invest in financial assets because you expect to accumulate wealth. This increase in wealth is the *return* or the reward for investing which is also the basis of investment performance.

5.1 What Is My Rate of Return?

More and more, "get rich overnight" investment schemes abound but in reality there are very few instant millionaires (exceptions include the state lottery winners and even they are not instant millionaires — proceeds are paid out as an annuity!). There are dinner time telephone calls from "boiler room operations" with investment scams that ask, "how would you like to double your money?," or "Invest in this stock and you are guaranteed to earn 500 percent on your money."

Guaranteed? By whom? If investments were paying these kinds of returns, operators of these scams would have invested in these projects and would be basking in the sun on the beaches of the south of France. Remember, nobody will sell anything for $1 when it can be sold for $5.

A number of warning flags should go up when confronted with these and other investment proposals. The first question to ask is:

"Is this promised rate of return reasonable as compared with similar investments?"

If it is not, it is an empty promise. In reality, it is difficult to measure the rate of return of certain investments such as common stock due to the fact that they may not pay dividends and that stock markets are

77

78   Chapter 5

volatile. However, by looking at historic rates of return for different types of investments, you can get a feeling for what to expect. Bear in mind that the past does not guarantee future results.

Karen Slater (1989a) quotes the rates of return for the following investments from studies done by Ibbotson Associates Inc. of Chicago:

Period of Investment	Stocks (S & P index)	Bonds L.T. U.S.	Treasury Bills
1926-1988	10%	4.4%	3.5%
1984-1988	15.4%	15%	7.1%
January-June 1989*	16.4%	13.1%	4.1%
Best Year	54% (1933)	40.4% (1982)	14.7% (1981)
Worst Year	–43% (1931)	–9.2% (1967)	0% (1938)

* Not an annualized rate

If a person had invested in stocks (approximating the basket of stocks in the S & P index), long-term U. S. bonds and T-bills in 1926 and reinvested the dividends and interest, the average annual returns through 1988 would have been 10 percent for stocks, 4.4 percent for bonds and 3.5 percent for T-bills. Returns earned by stocks for these periods are the greatest but stock markets tend to be the most volatile so investors can do very well in bull markets (a 54 percent return in 1933). Needless to say, bear markets can easily swing into the negative returns (–43 percent in 1931). Investing in stocks over long periods of time tends to average out the variability of the returns. Of course, if we know when the bull markets are going to occur, we would not have to bother about bear markets and having to average out the negative returns. Unfortunately, persons who can predict the future are few and far between.

In the 1980s, bond markets became increasingly volatile due to greater fluctuations in interest rates. This is evidenced by the 40.4 percent return in 1982.

It's important to keep these norms in mind before jumping into an investment which promises unreasonably high returns. It's quite natural to look for investments that give higher returns but when examining some of the theories on security prices, you'll quickly come to the conclusion that Wall Street gives nothing away.

There is a theory that financial markets are very efficient and competitive which, if true, would make it very difficult to consistently outperform the market. Efficient markets imply that security prices always reflect available information. Thus, a stock that is undervalued would be driven up in price by all investors who buy it and the returns for subsequent purchasers of this stock will be lower. Similarly, an overvalued stock would be sold which would drive the price down. Therefore, the market price of a security reflects its intrinsic value due to all known information. There will be few mispriced securities.

This being the case, the theory implies that investors cannot consistently outperform the market or consistently underperform the market. In other words, on average, investors do no better or worse than the market averages over an extended period of time. This is not to say that you cannot find securities which earn exceptional returns. For example, if you had bought MCI Corp. shares for $7 per share in 1984 and sold them in 1990 for $45 per share, you would have earned an abnormally large return. The theory of efficient markets implies that investors will not be able to consistently earn these kinds of returns.

In his book *A Random Walk Down Wall Street,* Burton G. Malkiel supports the efficient market theory by arguing that investors would do no better or no worse than the market averages if they chose their investments by throwing darts at the stock tables. Periodically, the *Wall Street Journal* publishes results that compare stocks picked by dart throwers and those by financial analysts. Stock picks of the dart throwers often outperform those of the analysts.

This all boils down to the fact that if the markets are so efficient, how can you "beat the markets?" It is this author's opinion that there are no known (legal) methods for "beating the markets." If there are some unknown methods, as soon as they become known to the public, they will no longer be successful because the advantages or inefficiencies they had exploited would be evened out by the market. Be very skeptical of schemes to beat the market.

Ivan Boesky showed that he could successfully beat the market; he also received a three-year prison sentence. Using inside information about companies which no one else had access to was very profitable for Ivan Boesky but insider trading is also illegal.

Many studies have been done on financial markets. The 1990 Nobel prize laureates for economics, Harry Markovitz and William Sharpe, have done work on financial markets which have had a profound effect.

Harry Markovitz's work pioneered what is now known as the modern portfolio theory. Concerned with the composition of assets that investors would select for their portfolios, Markovitz determined that the major properties of an asset of concern to investors are risk and return. By choosing a range of different assets for a portfolio, investors would be able to determine and control the total risk in that portfolio through variance analysis of each asset.

William Sharpe further developed Markovitz's approach into the model known as the capital asset pricing model (CAPM). In this model,

80   Chapter 5

the risk of portfolio theory can be broken down into two parts: *systematic risk* of an asset and *unsystematic risk* of an asset.

Systematic risk is similar to market risk in that the movement of the security's price is proportional to the movement of prices in the general market. Systematic risk is measured by the Greek letter *beta*. A stock with a beta coefficient of one indicates that if the market rises by 20 percent, this stock will go up in price by 20 percent. Increased diversification into many different stocks in a portfolio will not eliminate systematic risk — these stocks will not be immune to a downturn in the market.

Unsystematic risk encompasses all other types of risk pertaining to that security: business risk, financial risk, purchasing power risk — factors pertaining to that company that will affect its stock price. By diversifying one's assets in a portfolio, unsystematic risk can be eliminated.

Sharpe's model has evoked controversy which is still being debated. The implications of the CAPM are that the selection of high beta stocks in a portfolio is likely to produce above average returns in a bull market and, of course, below average returns in a bear market. According to the model, unsystematic risk can be eliminated through diversification even though the portfolio may have very high (unsystematic) risk assets. This evokes the question:

"Is it better to pursue high (unsystematic) risk, high return securities?"

5.2   The Greatest Return May Not Be the Best?

Since there are no known legal methods of beating the market, you could try your luck at gambling. If you go to the roulette tables, put your life savings into a chip and place it on the color red, what are the odds of winning? A roulette wheel is not evenly divided into red and black spaces — there may be one or two spaces which are neither color. You will, therefore, have a less than 50/50 chance of winning. The odds are stacked against you because you have a greater chance of losing your money. If you do win, you will receive an abnormally large return — 100 percent — but over many tries you cannot expect to win. In fact, the odds show that you will lose money if you persist. You can exclude gambling from your investments because you will not earn any money over the long run. The anticipated return does not justify the very real risk of losing your money.

As mentioned in earlier chapters, all investments bear some elements of risk. You do, however, expect to earn a positive return over a period of time. Conservative investments such as insured bank deposits

How Well Are My Investments Doing?   81

and Treasury bills, despite their assured returns, are not immune from purchasing power risks. Similarly, if you had invested in high yielding junk bonds issues in the 1980s, you may find that the current market value is considerably less than the amount of your initial investment. Investors who had avoided the stock market in the 1980s missed out on the high returns of a bull market. What becomes apparent is that higher returns are only earned from accepting greater risks. For instance, in the 1980s, many investors were lured into investing in futures by the advertised double and triple digit returns. Studies indicate that 90 percent of investors lose money in futures trading.

This chapter should shatter any notion of overnight get-rich investments! Investments with abnormally large returns are encumbered by very high levels of risk — which means that you could also lose your initial investments. Individual investors must decide whether additional returns warrant the additional risks. This is known as the risk-return trade off; you must choose the level of risk you feel comfortable with.

The work of Markovitz and Sharpe shows that there are ways to manage the levels of risk. Risk-averse investors should invest in many different types of assets in order to reduce the extremes of returns. In other words, it will be difficult to lose all money and conversely, it will be hard to treble one's return in a short period of time. Gains and losses in a diversified portfolio offset each other. Using Sharpe's model, risk-averse investors invest in assets with low beta coefficients.

The risk-neutral investor looks for investments which give the highest rates of return without regard for diversification.

The risk-seeker takes chances even if it means sacrificing expected returns.

Most investors are risk-averse and want to find investments which will give steady, positive, annual returns and the ability to sleep well at night. Increasing the rates of return earned from investments which still fall within acceptable risk levels enhance overall values for the investor due to the time value of money concept.

Consider the differences among the following three investments:

$100 per month is invested in A, B and C.

A)   A bank account paying 5 percent per annum compounded monthly;

B)   A Money Market Deposit Account paying 7 percent per annum compounded monthly;

C)   A Money Market Mutual Fund paying 8 percent per annum compounded monthly.

82   Chapter 5

	Rate	Future Value in 1 Year	Future Value in 5 Years	Future Value in 10 Years
A	5%	$1,228.11	$6,807.55	$15,561.50
B	7%	1,239.03	7,151.88	17,270.43
C	8%	1,245.22	7,355.35	18,335.48

Although the difference between the future values is not significant after one year, $17.11 ($1,245.22 − 1,228.11), by increasing the rate of return from 5 percent to 8 percent, the difference compounds to $2,773.98 ($18,335.48 − 15,561.50) in ten years. In this example, the level of risk has not increased appreciably from a bank deposit to a money market mutual fund. Even though a bank deposit has FDIC insurance and money market mutual funds do not, money market funds tend to invest in relatively safe investments such as Treasury bills, CDs and commercial paper.

The time value of money concept illustrates the importance of higher rates of return and with higher rates come increased levels of risk. You must then evaluate whether the additional returns are worth the additional risks. Therefore, choose investments that offer the highest rates of return for the level of risk that you are willing to bear.

5.3   How To Measure Rates of Return

Assume that you bought some common stock for $10,000 in January 1987, and sold it for $10,600 on December 29, 1988. What rate of return did you earn and is it a good rate of return?

The rate of return for the holding period can be calculated as follows:

$$\text{Rate of Return} = \frac{\text{Gain}}{\text{Purchase Price of the Stock}}$$

$$= \frac{600}{10,000}$$

$$= 6\%$$

The return is 6 percent for the holding period of two years, which can be annualized to 3 percent per year (6 percent/2). Thus, the average annual return is 3 percent. Whether this is a good or bad return depends on what the investor uses as a yardstick for comparison. For example, the rate of return can be compared with the stock market averages for those years. If the S & P Index had a negative 8 percent annual rate of

How Well Are My Investments Doing?   83

return for this same period, this was a superior investment; but if the market increased by 10 percent per year, this investment was inferior.

This is the simplest and easiest rate of return to calculate, and the formula can be expanded to include interest (for bonds) and dividends (for stocks).

$$\text{Rate of Return} = \frac{\text{Sale Price } - \text{ Purchase Price } + \text{ Interest or Dividends}}{\text{Purchase Price}}$$

If an investor bought stock for \$100, received dividends of \$5 and then sold the stock for \$150 at the end of five years, the return for five years is:

$$= \frac{150 - 100 + 5}{100}$$

$$= 55\%$$

The average annual return is 11 %

This return is also misleading because the time value of money is not taken into account. Dividends received each year will earn a return which is not considered in this average return. Similarly, the initial investment would also earn a return which will be compounded to equal \$150 in five years. In other words, if the \$100 had been invested in the bank, at what rate would it grow to \$150, bearing in mind that each year the interest earned on the principal is being reinvested? The true rate of return for this investment can be calculated using the following equation:

$$\begin{array}{c}\text{Purchase Price} \\ \text{of the Stock}\end{array} = \begin{array}{c}\text{Present Value of the} \\ \text{Dividends Discounted} \\ \text{at R\% for Five Years}\end{array} + \begin{array}{c}\text{Present Value of the} \\ \text{Sale Price Discounted at} \\ \text{R\% at the end of Five Years}\end{array}$$

Using present value tables or a financial calculator, this can be solved for the rate of return. This same formula may be used to determine the true rate of return of a bond. Therefore, this annual return of 11 percent is overstated and is really less per year when compounding is considered.

Inflation

Whether the true or average rate of return is used, consider the effects of inflation on the rate of return. If an investment earns 7 percent per annum and the rate of inflation is 5 percent, the real rate of return is only 2 percent. Thus, if inflation rises above 7 percent, investors will, to say

84   Chapter 5

the least, not be ecstatic at holding an investment that gives a zero percent
real rate of return. This is why the market prices of long-term bonds take
such a severe beating when inflation rises, because bondholders receive
fixed amounts of interest.

If you expect the rate of inflation to increase, you should choose
investments that will yield higher rates of return. This partially explains
why interest rates generally increase during inflationary times. To com-
bat inflation, the Federal Reserve Bank tightens credit which drives
interest rates up.

As shown in the previous chapter, investors tend to avoid long-term
fixed income securities (long-term debt) and look for short-term investments (such as money market accounts and T-bills) where rates of return
increase with rates of inflation during periods of rising interest rates.
Certain physical assets such as real estate tend to do very well during
inflationary times. Correspondingly, common stocks of companies
which have assets that increase in value during inflation will also do
well. It stands to reason that you try to protect yourselves from the
ravages of inflation by constructing portfolios of investments with expected rates of return that are higher than anticipated rates of inflation.

Taxes

It is not only inflation that causes returns to be diminished; there are
taxes as well. Interest and dividends are taxed as ordinary income. Capital
gains at the time of this writing are also taxed at ordinary tax rates,
although the capital gains provisions still remain in the Internal Revenue
Tax Code. This implies that if ordinary tax rates go up, capital gains
may then be taxed at special lower rates as was the case before the
changes to the Tax Code.

Although ordinary income tax rates have come down from the high
50 percent marginal tax brackets to the current 33 percent and 28 percent
brackets, taxes still take a significant bite out of returns. For instance, if
we look at the returns from the Ibbotson Associates Inc. study as quoted
by Slater (1989a), earlier in the chapter, we see the before tax returns:

	Stocks (S & P Index)	Bonds (L.T.U.S.)	Treasury Bills
1926-1988	10%	4.4%	3.5%

Taking tax rates out of these average annual returns by assuming
an average annual tax rate of 30 percent would give us the following
after tax returns:

	Stocks	**Bonds**	**Treasury Bills**
1926-1988	7% (10%-3%)	3.1% (4.4%-1.3%)	2.5% (3.5%-1%)

This may not appear at first glance to be so damaging: the average annual after tax return on stocks is reduced from 10 percent to 7 percent, bonds from 4.4 percent to 3 percent, and T-bills from 3.5 percent to 2.5 percent. However, when these diminished returns are compounded over the years, there is a considerable difference.

For instance, $1 compounded at 10 percent for twenty years equals $6.728;

$1 compounded at 7 percent for twenty years equals $3.87.

The future value of the after tax return is almost half the pre-tax amount when the time value of money is considered.

The damage is further compounded when the after tax return is adjusted for inflation and any sales commissions and administrative fees.

5.4   How Can You Improve Your Rates of Return?

From the Ibbotson Associates Inc. study and others, it is evident that stocks tend to give the highest rates of return over long periods of time followed by bonds and then Treasury bills. Before jumping to conclusions based on these studies that you can randomly invest all your money in stocks and earn 10 percent annually, you must realize that past returns may not be indicative of future returns. For instance, we may have a recession in the coming year which may send the market into negative returns. The 10-percent annual rate of return was averaged over sixty-three years. Over long periods of time, stocks tend to give the best returns because variations of the market are averaged out.

Small Company Stocks

Ibbotson and Brinson (1987) did a study comparing the returns of small company stocks with those of large company stocks over a sixty-year period. They found that small company stocks had average annual returns of 18 percent versus 12 percent for large company stocks. The risks were much higher for the small company stocks as shown by the standard

86   Chapter 5

deviation of 36 percent compared with 12 percent for the large companies.

Historically, small company stocks have produced greater returns than large company stocks but there are no guarantees that this will occur in the future. Secondly, it is hard for the individual to duplicate these results because individuals buy a few stocks whereas these studies are based on all the small company stocks on the market.

Two questions may now cross your mind:

"Which small and large companies stocks should I buy?" and "Does it make a difference which stocks I buy?"

The efficient market theory may not have aroused your enthusiasm since it shatters any thoughts of creating overnight wealth in the stock market. You are not alone! Security analysts and professional portfolio managers have not wholeheartedly supported the efficient market theory either.

The efficient market theory suggests that few investors will consistently beat the market averages over a long period of time, which then implies support for portfolios chosen by throwing darts as opposed to a carefully chosen portfolio. If prices are so efficiently set, one need not spend time and money employing a portfolio manager, especially since management fees reduce rates of returns. Active supporters of the efficient market theory have thus pursued the strategy of investing in index funds for both stocks and bonds where the portfolios replicate the S & P Index for stocks and the Shearson Lehman Index for bonds. Fees for these funds are relatively low because analysts do not need to be employed to choose stocks and bonds and transaction fees and commissions are also low due to the buy-hold strategy. The major problem with a randomly selected portfolio chosen from throwing darts is that risks connected with individual stocks in the portfolio are ignored.

For those of you who feel that the efficient market theory is not equally efficient with regard to pricing all stocks — especially some of the smaller lesser known stocks — there is a role for fundamental analysis. Fundamental analysis involves financial analysis of companies to find those stocks whose prices are undervalued. Even though many studies have shown that few financial analysts and portfolio managers can consistently do better than the market averages, there are enough anomalies in the results of these studies to continue the search for undervalued stocks.

Many investors look for patterns for picking superior stocks to buy. They study the historical data and plot the prices of the stock on charts which produce all kinds of shapes, the head and shoulders being one of them. From this, they will determine the optimal prices to buy or sell the stock, by projecting the past information into the future. This is known as *technical analysis*, the study of the historical behavior of the market and of individual securities.

Several different technical approaches such as the *odd lot theory* — attempt to predict changes in the direction of market performance. The odd lot theory suggests that small investors are weak and emotional as compared with professional investors. Thus, when small investors begin to purchase stocks (odd lot purchases will increase), there will be a change in the direction of the market because small investors only begin to buy when the market is near its peak. During declining markets, small investors start to sell their stocks at close to the bottom of the market Odd lot purchases and sales can be found in the daily financial newspapers There is very little empirical evidence to support the odd lot theory.

It is not only small investors who may often be wrong but the *contrarian* method of picking stocks suggests that financial advisors are often wrong. According to this method, when advisors and analysts are bullish, it is time to sell your securities. Similarly, when financial advisors are bearish, it is time to buy securities. Although there is some support for this theory, it is almost bizarre to go against those who spend their lives studying the market.

There are many who use *insider trading* to determine whether to buy or sell a particular stock. Such investors monitor the buying and selling of stocks by officers, directors and large shareholders of corporations. These insiders have access to privileged information and are required to report their buying and selling transactions to the SEC. When insiders buy more stock than they are selling, it would be considered a bullish sign for that stock. The opposite is also true — when insider selling is greater than insider buying, it is a bearish signal. Several studies support this method as a means of picking superior stocks. The *Insiders Chronicle* and the *Wall Street Journal* report insider transactions.

Other than studying insider trading, there is little academic support for finding superior investments through technical analysis. In fact, Burton Malkiel feels that stock prices tend to move randomly and are not related to the previous day's prices. You could do as well by purchasing a randomly selected portfolio of stocks. Mr. Malkiel has conceded that there are exceptions to the random walk model, but argues that these profits will be negated by the transaction costs of having to buy and sell the securities (Angrist and Dorfman, 1990).

The overall importance of the efficient market theory is that:

- investors will not consistently earn superior returns from their investments; and

88   Chapter 5

- the only way to increase returns would be to invest in riskier investments.

This then leads to the importance of the construction of a portfolio of investments that will be compatible with the investor's overall level of risk. This can be accomplished through diversification which can eliminate some of the unnecessary risks. Furthermore, returns can be improved through the reduction of taxes, investment fees and commissions.

Interest on most municipal bonds is exempt from federal taxes and interest on U.S. obligations is exempt from state and local taxes. Investors should consider whether there are any advantages to holding municipal bonds and should also look into individual retirement accounts (IRAs) even though they are no longer deductible at the higher levels of income. The advantage of such accounts is that the interest, dividends and capital gains are not taxed until withdrawals are made at retirement. The merits of these accounts should be discussed with competent tax advisors because there is an excise tax which the government has imposed on withdrawals from retirement accounts above a certain level of income, as well as a penalty for withdrawal of the funds before retirement.

Reducing or eliminating fees and sales commissions can increase returns significantly. Compare the commissions charged by your broker with those charged by competitive brokers in the area. Often full service brokers will discount their commissions if asked, due to the increasing competition from discount brokerage firms. Since many brokers make their money buying and selling securities, they have an incentive to advise their clients to trade more than they should. This is called *churning* which is the buying and selling of securities at a rate which is not justified by their returns. Be very careful about giving your broker the discretion to trade on your behalf — unless you trust your broker implicitly and are convinced that he/she can beat the market!

One way to reduce the costs of churning through the active buying and selling of securities is to invest in a stock or bond mutual fund. "No-load" mutual funds do not charge sales commissions whereas regular "load" funds will charge a commission every time shares are bought or sold. Brokers don't handle "no-load" funds because they don't receive any commissions. The reduction of transaction fees and sales commissions can increase overall returns over an extended period of time.

The emphasis in this chapter has been to choose investments with compatible levels of risk and return. As discussed, diversification of assets is essential to minimize risks at a particular level of return. The composition of your portfolio is based on your goals and expected risks and returns of assets. Changes in the portfolio will then be made as your

How Well Are My Investments Doing?   89

goals and circumstances change. For instance, with a longer investment period, there can be a greater emphasis on stocks in the portfolio.

Gregory, a money manager in San Francisco, estimates the risks of losing money on an investment in a basket of stocks resembling the S & P Index, at 3-4 percent over a ten-year period, versus 15 percent over a three-year period and 30 percent over a one-year period (Earl C. Gottschalk Jr. and Barbara Donnelly, 1989).

Returns from the Ibbotson studies confirm that over the long term, stocks outperformed bonds and Treasury bills. In fact, bond and Treasury bill returns, when adjusted for inflation and taxes, showed dismal returns. To earn higher returns over extended periods of time, investors should weight a greater portion of their portfolios towards stocks and pursue a long-term buy and hold strategy which minimizes commissions and improves overall returns. Over shorter periods of time, stocks become riskier.

5.5   Caveats for Investors

There is a direct relationship between rates of return and risk and before investing, you should consider the following questions:

- Is the expected rate of return for the investment abnormally high as compared with similar investments? Is this based on past performance?

- Is this investment based on sound business sense? If not, forget the whole thing.

- Is there pressure to invest immediately or put some money up front? Be cautious of schemes which require you to act quickly.

- Who are the principals? If they are not known to you, have them checked out, especially with regard to their previous operations. Check if they have ever been involved in bankruptcy.

- Are there financial statements? If so, are they audited? Check the auditor's report for qualified or adverse opinions.

- Can you afford to lose the money that you invest in this operation? If not, don't invest.

- Is there a guarantee? Can this be verified? Guaranteed by whom? Guaranteed by a company does not mean much if the company goes bankrupt and has no assets.

90   Chapter 5

- Has this investment been offered to you over the phone by someone you don't know or don't know very well? Never invest because of a telephone call.

- Always check every detail before you invest. If there is not enough time, look for something else to invest in.

- If you do invest, do not put additional money in to "help out" or for any other irrational reason. Keep your investment small.

Bear in mind that with the efficient market theory, very few investors consistently beat the market averages over a long period of time and the greater the return the greater the risk involved.

The Trader's Lament aptly sums up the investor's dilemma:

> Buy and you'll be sorry
> Sell and you'll regret
> Hold and you will worry
> Do nothing and you'll fret.

CHAPTER 6
OVERVIEW OF CREDIT

Imagine the following scenario:

Depositors wait for six hours in a long line outside a bank, not because it is about to go out of business but to invest in a special five-year bank deposit which reinvests the interest. Interest and principal will only be received at the end of five years and the effective yield is 9.6 percent.

Yes, this is real and no, the place is not the United States of America. This happened in Japan where older Japanese investors took advantage of the higher rates offered by the "wide" bonds of Japanese banks.

The decade of the 1980s was geared to abundant credit. The money supply of all the industrialized nations, including Germany and Japan, grew considerably. In the U.S, the money supply almost doubled in the decade. With the increasing pool of money to lend, lenders looked for clever ways to find borrowers. They certainly found them: one daily newspaper reported on a thirteen-year old who had succeeded in obtaining a credit card! Borrowers were ecstatic. In the U.S., individuals, companies, federal, state and local governments all said "yes" to more borrowing.

The use of consumer credit has soared and seems to be a way of life for many Americans. In fact, the American economy has often been called a credit economy. Consumers buy homes, cars, major appliances and even clothing, food and entertainment on credit; its an important way of life.

Opinions differ as to what use of credit is "appropriate." Before deciding how much credit is appropriate, it is important to look at both the reasons for borrowing and the costs of credit.

6.1   Reasons for Consumer Borrowing

Why use credit? It's cheaper to pay cash for everything — the interest and service charges incurred when using someone else's money would be eliminated. However, many of us may not have enough cash to buy large ticket items and it may take too long to save for the purchase. By using credit, you are able to enhance your standard of living by increasing

your current purchasing power. Simply put, you can obtain large ticket items immediately instead of waiting.

You may be forced to borrow due to unforeseen emergency situations or because you do not have enough in your savings accounts for these contingencies. There are many types of emergencies (medical, dental, casualty losses, etc.) where consumer loans may be necessary.

Some people borrow so that they can live the "good life" now. They finance vacations, luxury goods, impulse buying and entertainment. This way of life can become habit forming and difficult to break out of. It provides immediate gratification but can lead to problems later. After the vacation, there is the mountain of debt to be dealt with. This may mean that future sacrifices will have to be made in order to repay the loans and the finance charges. Even though debt provides instant gratification, it actually decreases total purchasing power due to the finance charges that need to be paid.

Credit cards are often used as a convenient way to purchase anything and everything. With the use of credit cards, you have the use of

Overview of Credit   93

the goods without having to pay for them immediately. If the payment is made in full during the grace period, which is a short period between the billing date and the payment date, finance charges can be avoided. In this case, you have the use of someone else's money for a short period of time until the debt is paid.

Many people borrow money to use for investments. If borrowed through brokerage firms, this is called investing on margin. The margin requirement, set by the Federal Reserve, is the percentage amount that you must put up in cash and the rest may be borrowed. Using borrowed funds to invest with could lead to problems if the investment does not appreciate more than the interest costs of the borrowed funds. Of course, if the investment does well, the rate of return is greater due to the fact that you have invested less money. Table 6.1 gives an example of using margin funds. All in all, it is a risky policy to borrow money to use for investment purposes.

Consumer interest is no longer tax deductible which means that the Internal Revenue Service no longer shields part of your interest expense. Before the Tax Reform Act of 1986, many people rationalized the benefits of being able to deduct all their consumer interest expenses before taxes.

Since the gradual phasing out of the tax deductibility of consumer interest through 1990, however, you should be aware that consumer debt will now cost you more in after tax dollars. Benjamin Franklin's words take on a new meaning: "He who goes a borrowing, goes a sorrowing."

You should try to stay out of consumer debt. Currently, mortgage interest and investment interest are tax deductible with certain restrictions. However, changes to the Tax Code are ongoing and before taking on new debt, you should check with your tax advisor as to the deductibility of the interest.

It is very tempting to borrow and lenders make it extremely easy. Those in the habit of borrowing may become so overburdened with debt that when an emergency arises they may not be able to obtain a loan for the funds that they need.

Before deciding the level of credit appropriate for you, it is important to look at the different types of credit and their costs.

6.2   The Types of Credit and Their Costs

There are four types of credit:

- Open-end;
- Cash loan;

94   Chapter 6

Table 6.1   Comparison of Returns Earned on Cash and Margin Purchase

Assume investor X buys 100 shares of IBM Corporation at $110 per share. The margin requirement is 50% and the brokerage firm charges interest at 10% per year. Investor Y also buys 100 shares of IBM Corporation at $110 per share. After one year both investors X and Y sell their 100 shares at $130 per share.

	Investor Y Cash Purchase	Investor X Margin Purchase
Selling Price	$13,000	$13,000
Cost	$11,000	$11,000
Profit	$ 2,000	$ 2,000
Investment	$11,000	$ 5,500
Rate of Return	18.18% ($2,000/$11,000)	26.36% (*$1,450/$5,500)

* Investor X borrowed 50% of the purchase price $5,500 from the brokerage firm. The finance charge is $550 (10% × $5,500). Investor X will pay the $550 out of the profit which means that the net profit is $1,450 ($2,000 − $550).

Investor X has increased the rate of return through borrowing funds. However, the reverse occurs if the stock price falls: the percentage loss will be greater with the use of borrowed funds.

Assume that the stock price falls to $90 at the end of the year.

	Investor Y Cash Purchase	Investor X Margin Purchase
Selling Price	$ 9,000	$ 9,000
Cost	$11,000	$11,000
Profit	($2,000)	($2,000)
(Percentage Loss)	(18.18%) ($2,000/$11,000)	(46.36%) ($2,550/$5,500)

- Sales (installment) loan;

- Mortgage Loan.

Open-End Credit

Open-end credit involves the use of credit cards and charge accounts. These are "open-ended" because you decide how much credit (within the credit limit set by the lender) to use and when to use it. You have the flexibility to pay the entire amount of the charge when billed or, on the other extreme, pay a minimum amount per month over a period of time.

Credit Cards are offered by banks and financial institutions, retail stores and oil companies. There is a wide variety of *credit cards* to choose from. In fact, credit card issuers have been very creative with their new enhancements to entice you to choose their cards. For example, most gold cards offer buyer protection packages and extended warranties on goods purchased with the cards.

Besides the waiving of the annual fee, however, there are other factors to consider in choosing a credit card — range of acceptance, the interest rates charged, the length of the grace period (the time between the billing date and the payment date) and the other enhancement packages.

If you are in the habit of paying your credit card bills *in full* every month, then choosing a credit card which has no annual fee and a grace period becomes important. However, if you are not in the habit of paying your credit card bills in full, the interest rates charged become important. Interest rates charged by credit card issuers can vary by as much as 6 to 8 percent. Some banks charge more than 20 percent — by shopping around, however, it is possible to find interest rates in the 12- to 15-percent range, possibly even lower. Bear in mind that even a 12 percent per annum rate works out to 1 percent per month on the unpaid balance — still a substantial rate. Be aware that some issuers of low interest credit cards may not include a grace period.

If you sometimes pay your balances in full and other times run up a balance, you should carry two types of cards: a no annual fee card and a second low interest rate credit card.

Other ways to beat the high cost of credit cards include considering bank loans, home equity loans and loans on your life insurance policies. For example, a purchase on your credit card which charges 16 to 20 percent could be compared to a twenty-four or thirty-six month unsecured personal loan from a local bank. Chances are the unsecured bank loan rate will be less. This is not to suggest that you take out two- or three-year loans to pay for short-lived goods and services, such as fancy clothes, a night out at an elegant restaurant, etc. If a purchase is for a durable good such as furniture or an appliance, however, it may be appropriate to check the costs of alternate sources of credit before going straight to a high interest credit card. Before using any credit, always determine whether the benefits of the purchase exceed the costs of the credit.

96   Chapter 6

The total cost of a credit card is the interest charge plus any annual fees. The interest charge can be assessed in two ways:

- The interest rate is multiplied by the *unpaid* balance in the account. For example, if you bought something for $300 and pay $100 when the credit card statement comes, you have a $200 unpaid balance. If the interest rate is 18 percent, the monthly rate is then 1.5 percent. The total interest charge which would be added to the outstanding balance the next month would be $3:

$$1.5 \text{ percent} \times \$200 = \$3$$

- Some credit card issuers charge interest on the average daily balance from the statement date to the next statement date. Assume that you have a $200 outstanding balance from the last month and you add $100 to the outstanding balance this month. If you pay $100 twenty days after the grace period, your average daily balance is calculated as follows:

$200 × 30 days	6,000
$100 × 20 days	2,000
	8,000

Average daily balance	=	$266.67 (8,000/30)
Interest charge	=	$4 (1.5% × $266.67)

It is important to know which method is being used to calculate interest charges. By not paying credit card balances in full, interest charges can amount to substantial sums at the high rates of interest charged. This decreases future purchasing power so credit cards must be used carefully. See Table 6.2 for a summary of what you should know about credit cards.

Charge cards are offered by different types of businesses, such as department stores, mainly to facilitate sales. Stores will open up accounts, depending on creditworthiness and allow purchases up to the credit limits set. If payments are made in full during the grace period (ten to thirty days after the statement date) finance charges can be avoided. If payments are not made in full, finance charges in the range of 1 percent to 2 percent per month will be incurred on the unpaid balances — similar to those of credit cards. Unpaid balances can be extended over several months which means that finance charges make up a part of each payment until the balance is paid off.

Overview of Credit 97

Table 6.2 What You should Know about Credit Cards

1. If you have no credit cards and want to establish credit, apply for a gasoline credit card or a department store card. Pay your bills promptly to establish a good credit record and then apply for bank credit cards.

2. Shop around for the credit card with the best terms.

3. Sign your credit cards as soon as you receive them and keep them in a safe place.

4. Keep a list of your credit card numbers and the telephone numbers of the issuing companies.

5. If you lose your card or if it is stolen, telephone the credit card issuer immediately. Follow this up with a certified letter notifying the issuer of the loss or theft. If you do this before the card is used, you will not be liable for any of the unauthorized charges. Under federal law, if you follow this procedure the most you will be liable for is $50.

6. Never give your credit card account number to anyone unless it is for a legitimate purchase. Be especially wary of callers wanting a credit card number in order to verify that you are eligible for a prize.

7. Never put your address or telephone number on charge card receipts. You do not want additional information falling into the wrong hands. Similarly, never write your charge card numbers on your checks.

8. When paying by credit card, never let your credit card out of sight (so that extra imprints are made of your card). Ask for the carbons and destroy them. Never sign a blank credit card receipt where the figures are filled in later.

9. Keep your receipts to verify the amounts of the charges on your monthly statements. If you find discrepancies, notify the credit card issuer in writing. You will not have to pay the disputed amount until the discrepancy is settled and interest charges will not accrue on disputed amounts.

10. Shop around for the credit card with the terms that suit your needs best.

Open-end credit should be used wisely. The most effective management of your money is to use open-end credit for purchases and then to pay the bills in full without incurring any finance charges. This way

98   Chapter 6

you have the use of someone else's money for the period before paying for the purchase. Why pay 1 or 2 percent per month to use someone else's money when your savings and investments only earn in the range of .5 to .9 percent per month?

Cash Loans

There are various reasons for obtaining cash loans as opposed to open-end credit which is used primarily for purchases. For instance, cash loans could be made to consolidate all other high cost debts for the purchase of goods or services, for home improvements, for tuition, for emergencies, etc. The maturities of cash loans can vary from a few days to several years. Cash loans are often taken out for the duration of a few days to supplement funds in the buying and selling of a primary residence. This happens when a buyer settles on a second house a few days before the selling of the first house. Thus, a cash loan is taken out to pay for the new house and is then repaid when the settlement takes place on the old house. Of course, to make it worthwhile for lenders, the finance charges will generally be higher for these short-term loans.

Loans can be *unsecured* or *secured*. An unsecured loan is one where the lender only has the assurance that you will repay the loan. Thus, in order to qualify for an unsecured loan, you must have a good credit record and a sufficient source of income. Since the lender bears the greater risk of repayment, the rates of interest charged on unsecured loans tend to be higher than those for secured loans.

A *secured* loan is one where you provide additional security (pledging an asset or having someone else cosign the loan) in order to get the loan. The lender will consider your creditworthiness and the additional security before granting the loan. If an asset is pledged, the lender will evaluate it as follows: can the asset be resold? If so, for how much? Will this amount cover the loan?

If the loan is cosigned, the lender will evaluate the cosignor's credit record, because if you default, the lender will expect the cosignor to repay the loan. (Do not be in a hurry to be a cosignor of a loan — you can quickly become liable for the borrower's debts.)

The advantages of a secured loan over an unsecured loan are that the interest rates are generally lower, the loan amounts are greater and the lengths of the loans are longer. Proceed with caution with a secured loan because if you default on it, the asset pledged will be lost or if cosigned, the cosignor will want to be repaid.

Sources of Consumer Loans The major sources of cash loans are banks, savings and loan associations, credit unions and consumer finance companies. There are other lenders such as brokerage firms, life insurance companies, pawnbrokers and loan brokers.

Banks and *Savings and Loan Associations* (S & Ls) offer many types of loans and are competitive in their rates. If you have an established credit record, you should shop around for the most favorable terms.

Credit Unions provide savings and lending services to their members. For members, this is a good source of credit since credit union finance charges tend to be on the low end of the scale. If you have a good credit record, you should compare the interest rates of loans offered by credit unions, banks and S & Ls for the best set of terms.

If you have a limited or poor credit record, *consumer finance companies* may be the place to start looking. Consumer finance companies often make loans to borrowers without established credit histories. Because of this, most loans are made on a secured basis. States regulate consumer finance companies as to the maximum amounts they can lend and the maximum rates of interest they can charge. Interest rates and financial charges tend to be higher than from other sources — if you have a good credit record, compare the terms to those offered from other institutions.

You might also consider loans from other specialized sources. Some *brokerage firms* make cash loans which can be used for purposes other than buying investments. A brokerage firm may be a good source for a loan if you have made many investments through the firm.

If you have accumulated cash values on your life insurance policies (whole life, universal life, etc.), you can borrow against those cash values from your *life insurance company*. Life insurance companies tend to be an overlooked source of credit. When you borrow against your own accumulated cash values, you do not need to provide your credit record to the insurance company in order to qualify for the loan because you are borrowing against your own cash values. All that is required is completion of a form from your insurance company. Interest charges are often added to your insurance premiums. The interest rates charged by insurance companies tend to be very competitive and may be the lowest when compared with other sources. This is because the insurance company bears no risk — the money borrowed is your own money.

Borrowers who cannot obtain loans from traditional sources may turn to pawnbrokers and/or loan brokers. *Pawnbrokers* or pawnshops will give loans in return for pledging certain assets. Generally, they do

100   Chapter 6

not lend more than 50 percent of the appraised values of the pledged asset due to the high number of defaults and their finance charges are extremely high.

Loan brokers act as intermediaries in that they bring borrowers and lenders together. Loan brokers do not provide the loans. Instead, supposedly, many have access to "long lists" of lenders who are willing and able to lend to borrowers who have no other access to loans. Loan brokers charge fees (generally up front) before bringing borrowers and lenders together and if the loans materialize, the finance charges are extremely high. During recessions and credit crunches, there seem to be more scams involving loan brokers, where fraudulent loan brokers collect advance fees without producing the promised loans. Generally, loan brokers should be avoided. If you cannot get a loan from any other source and you need money desperately to help you out of your credit crunch, see a credit counselor. One more loan will more than likely not solve your problems.

What Is the Cost of a Consumer Loan?

When in the market for borrowing money, do not accept the first offer without checking the terms of competing institutions. In order to compare the different terms, you need to be able to work out the real cost of the loan. Since 1969, lenders have been required to disclose the annual percentage rate (APR) of interest and the actual amount of finance charges in dollars. The APR is the true cost of the loan, determined by dividing the total finance charges by the loan balance. By comparing the annual percentage rates of the competing loans, you can choose the loan with the lowest cost.

Single payment loans can have interest charged using the simple interest method, or the discounted method.

Simple Interest Using simple interest, the finance charge is calculated by multiplying the stated annual interest rate by the amount of the loan. For example, if you borrow $2,000 from the Friendly Bank for two years at 11 percent simple interest, the interest expense or finance charge is $220 per year:

Annual Interest Expense	$11\% \times \$2,000$
	$\underline{\$220}$
Annual Percentage Rate	$220/2,000$
	$\underline{11\%}$

When simple interest is used, the APR is equal to the stated interest rate.

Discounted Interest

Using discounted interest, the lender will deduct the finance charges from the loan in advance. For example, if the Friendly Bank gave you a single payment discounted loan of $2,000 at 11 percent for two years, the finance charge is $220 per year (calculated in the same way as the simple interest method). The difference, however, is that you will receive only $1,560, as the finance charge of $440 ($220 per year for two years) is deducted from the loan of $2,000. The true cost or APR for the loan is 14.1 percent:

Annual Percentage Rate	220/1,560
	14.1%

Discounted interest results in a higher annual percentage rate than using the simple interest method.

Sales Loan (Installment Loans)

Sales or installment loans are used mainly to buy consumer goods such as cars, furniture and appliances. Generally, sales loans are made by the merchants and no cash changes hands. When you buy merchandise using a sales loan, you receive the merchandise in return for a promise to pay regular periodic amounts of interest and principal. You may also have to make a cash down payment for part of the purchase price. The merchandise becomes security for the loan.

The amounts of the loans have wide ranges, from under $100 to over $30,000, as do the finance rates, 10 percent to 30 percent per annum. These rates change with market changes in interest rates.

When you buy using installment loans, you should shop around at different dealers for the best terms, including the terms of the installment loans. This is especially important for large ticket items, because by accepting the first deal you may end up paying considerably more than if you had shopped around. You can always go back to the first dealer if the terms were the best. Dealers of large ticket items are in the business of selling and will be just as happy to serve you the following day. By having shopped around, you know that you are getting the best terms.

Although a sales loan may originate between you and the dealer, there are often three parties involved. The dealer may not want to wait

102   Chapter 6

through the duration of the loan to receive all of his/her money. Instead, the dealer may sell the sales loan to a bank, finance company or other lending institution to receive the cash at the time of sale.

Some of these lending institutions offer rebates to dealers for encouraging the use of sales loans to prospective buyers. It may be in the dealer's interest to choose lenders who offer the greatest rebates rather than the lowest finance charges.

Besides shopping for the best sales loan terms, you also need to consider the dealer's reputation and ability to service or fix a defective appliance. If you have a problem, send certified letters documenting your dispute to both the dealer and the financial lender and then stop making payments until the problem is rectified.

Of course, if there is no problem and you stop making your regular payments, the goods/appliance may be legally repossessed. The repossessed goods can then be resold to recover the balance of the outstanding loan. If the proceeds from the resale are less than the amount of the outstanding loan, the borrower will be liable for the difference.

If you foresee problems in not being able to afford the monthly payments, discuss them with the lender. The lender may be sympathetic and lower the amount of the payments or allow you to sell the asset in order to repay the loan.

Try to avoid repossession because your credit record will be jeopardized and the repossessed goods may not be sold for the highest price. This means you could still be liable for an amount that falls short of the outstanding loan balance.

What is the Cost of a Sales Loan?   Cash is the cheapest way to buy something but for most of us, using sales or cash loans may be the only alternatives. When using sales loans, it is important to know the real cost of interest. Lenders of installment/sales loans can use the *pre-computed interest* method, or the *add-on* method, for calculating interest.

Pre-Computed Interest or Effective Interest Method   An install-ment/sales loan requires that you make regular periodic payments of interest and principal. Under this method, the total interest is computed at the outset of the loan. Table 6.3 gives an example of a $1,000, 12 percent, one-year installment loan.

The total pre-computed interest is $66.20 and the monthly payments of $88.85 are due on the last day of every month. Table 6.3 shows how the payments are divided into principal and interest. The interest remains the same even if payments are made before the due date. If

Overview of Credit   103

Table 6.3   Installment Loan

Monthly Payment $88.85   Interest rate   12.000%   Term in Months   12

Month/Year	Payment	Mo. Interest	Mo. Principal	Principal Bal.
Beginning				1,000.00
JAN 1991	88.85	10.00	78.85	921.15
FEB 1991	88.85	9.21	79.64	841.51
MAR 1991	88.85	8.42	80.43	761.08
APR 1991	88.85	7.61	81.24	679.84
MAY 1991	88.85	6.80	82.05	597.79
JUN 1991	88.85	5.98	82.87	514.92
JUL 1991	88.85	5.15	83.70	431.22
AUG 1991	88.85	4.31	84.54	346.68
SEP 1991	88.85	3.47	85.38	261.30
OCT 1991	88.85	2.61	86.24	175.06
NOV 1991	88.85	1.75	87.10	87.96
DEC 1991	88.85	0.89	87.96	0.00
Totals	1,066.20	66.20	1,000.00	

Number of Months Printed: 12

payments are made after the due date, however, a late penalty will be assessed. Most lenders give a grace period of up to fourteen days before the late penalty fee is charged. The outstanding loan balance declines every month by the amount of the principal reduction which is the greater part of the monthly payment in this loan schedule.

The APR is the same as the stated rate for this method because the interest is calculated using the stated rate, multiplied by the outstanding loan balance. When applying for installment loans, always check to see if there is a pre-payment penalty — a fee imposed if you pay the loan off early. Try to avoid loans with pre-payment penalty clauses because if you do come into some additional money, you could pre-pay your loan without incurring additional charges.

The *simple interest method* is a variant of the pre-computed interest method. Using the simple interest method, you pay simple interest on the outstanding balance only for the time that the money is used. For example, using the same loan of $1,000 with a 12-percent simple interest

104   Chapter 6

calculation and a term of twelve months, the monthly interest expense is determined by when payments are received. Monthly payments of $88.85 will be the same but interest expense is determined by the number of days before the payment is received.

Assume that the first payment is made after twenty days, the second after thirty-six days and the third after twenty-one days. Table 6.4 shows the amortization schedule for the first three payments.

The interest expense of $6.57 for January is calculated as follows (1,000 × 20 days × 12 percent/365). The principal reduction of $82.38 is the monthly payment of $88.95 minus the interest expense of $6.57. For February, the interest expense is $10.87 ($917.62 × 36 days × 12 percent/365). The February interest expense of $10.87 is greater than the interest expense using the pre-computed method, because there is a thirty-six day lapse since the first payment. In March, the interest expense is less than under the pre-computed method because the interest period is twenty-one days as opposed to the regular thirty or thirty-one day cycle used for the pre-computed method.

The advantage of a simple interest loan is that if you make your payments before the due dates, especially at the beginning part of the loan when the principal balance is the highest, your interest charges will be lower than they would be using the pre-computed method.

However, with simple interest loans, you should always check to see that there are no restrictions to making early payments. This negates the advantage of the simple interest loan. Also, you should check to see how late payments are assessed and whether there are any late payment penalties.

The Add-on Method   The add-on method of computing interest on an installment loan results in a higher APR than the stated rate. Sup-

Table 6.4   Installment Loan—Simple Interest Method

Monthly Payment $88.95   Interest Rate   12%   Term 12 Months

Month	Days between Payment	Interest Expense (.000329 per day)	Principal Reduction	Balance
				$1,000.00
Jan	20	6.57	82.38	917.62
Feb	36	10.87	78.08	839.54
Mar	21	5.80	83.15	756.39

Overview of Credit 105

pose you get an installment loan of $1,000 with a 12 percent add-on rate for one year, the total interest expense is calculated as follows:

$$\text{Interest Expense} = \$1,000 \times 12\%$$
$$= \$\underline{120}$$

Table 6.5 shows the first four months of the amortization schedule for the add-on method.

The total interest is added to the loan amount and then divided by twelve to get the monthly payment of $93.33 [(1,000 + 120)/12]. With this method, the monthly interest expense is $10 even though the loan balance declines with each payment. As you can see, the true interest rate is higher than the 12 percent stated rate because the borrower is still paying $10 per month in interest when the loan balance has declined. There are actuarial tables to determine the APRs of the add-on method but the use of the following formula will approximate the APR:

$$\text{APR} = \frac{2 \times M \times I}{P(n + 1)}$$

where M = payment periods in the year
$\quad\quad$ I = Total Interest Charge
$\quad\quad$ P = Initial amount of the Loan
$\quad\quad$ n = total number of payments

The APR for this 12 percent add-on loan is

$$\text{APR} = \frac{2 \times 12 \times 120}{1,000(12 + 1)}$$

$$= \underline{22.2\%}$$

Table 6.5   Installment Loan—Add on Method

Monthly Payment $93.33   Interest Rate   12%   Term 12 Months

Month	Payment	Interest	Principal Reduction	Balance
				$1,000.00
Jan	93.33	10	83.33	916.67
Feb	93.33	10	83.33	833.34
Mar	93.33	10	83.33	750.01
Apr	93.33	10	83.33	666.68

106   Chapter 6

The lender is required by federal law to disclose the APR. If you see that the APR is significantly higher than the stated rate, you know that this is an add-on method installment loan. Of the three methods used to calculate interest charges, the add-on method results in the highest interest charges and the greatest APR.

By understanding how the finance charges are determined on installment loans, you will be in a better position to negotiate the installment loan that is best for you.

Mortgage Loans

Most personal residences in the U.S. are bought with the assistance of mortgage financing. The borrower (mortgagor) borrows the money to buy the home which is the security for the debt and promises to make regular payments of principal and interest to the lender (mortgagee). Most mortgages are made by financial institutions such as banks, S & L Associations or mortgage institutions; in some cases mortgages are made by individuals.

Types of Mortgages   The types of mortgages offered today have changed from the original conventional fixed rate mortgages that were offered in the 1950s and 1960s. Conventional fixed rate mortgages are still offered with maturities of fifteen, twenty, twenty-five and thirty years but there are now adjustable rate mortgages (ARMs) and many hybrids in between.

Conventional fixed rate mortgages are the oldest type of mortgages offered by lenders. The interest rate is fixed at the time that the loan is negotiated. The maturities of the loans vary (fifteen, twenty, twenty-five, or thirty years) but they all require equal monthly payments over the lives of the mortgages. Over the last five years, lenders have offered fifteen-year mortgages with slightly lower interest rates (1/4 to 1/2 percent less) than those of the thirty-year maturities.

The advantages of fixed rate mortgages are that the amounts of the payments will not change over the lives of the mortgages and all financial institutions offer this type of mortgage. Disadvantages are that to get a conventional fixed rate mortgage, the required down payment is generally a greater percentage than for other types of mortgages and secondly, the interest rate will be higher than an adjustable rate mortgage.

All mortgages have different conditions which you should understand before accepting the mortgage:

- *Points* are fees in percentage points of the mortgage which raise the cost of the mortgage. Most mortgage lenders charge these fees; you should shop around at different lending institutions comparing the interest rate and the number of points charged. Some institutions may quote the same interest rate but with less points. For example, if you obtain a 10 percent $100,000 mortgage with three points, this would be an additional $3,000 fee. This would increase the effective interest rate of the loan above.

- *Prepayment Penalty* is a fee or penalty for repaying a mortgage before it matures. You do *not* want this clause because if you decide to sell your house before the mortgage is paid off or refinance at a lower rate, you will have to pay a fee.

- *Balloon Payment* is a large cash payment due at a specified time before the maturity of the mortgage. For example, if you have a twenty year $100,000 mortgage which has a balloon payment of $40,000 at the end of ten years, you will have to come up with this amount of cash halfway through your mortgage. Unless you have unlimited sources of cash available to meet this type of payment, you are better off without a balloon payment clause in your mortgage.

- *Acceleration Clause* requires the payment of the loan in full if any of the monthly payments are sixty to ninety days late. If you have an acceleration clause, make sure that you can pay your monthly payments and that they are sent in on time.

In addition to conventional fixed rate mortgages, there are *FHA* and *VA* fixed rate mortgages. FHA (Federal Housing Authority) loans are available to the public whereas VA (Veterans Administration) loans are only available to veterans. The loans are not made by these government agencies. Instead, the FHA insures the loans, allowing buyers to buy houses with smaller down payments than those required with conventional mortgages. If the buyer defaults on the mortgage, the FHA will pay the unpaid balance to the lender. Such insurance will cost the buyer a few percentage points of the mortgage, payable either at the inception of the loan or with the payments spread over the life of the loan.

VA loans, available only to qualified veterans, are guaranteed by the Veterans Administration. A borrower of a VA loan may have to make a small down payment, and interest rates are generally lower than market rates for similar length mortgages. However, the use of points by the lender of the VA guaranteed loan will increase the overall cost of the loan. On VA loans, the seller (of the property) generally pays the points while the buyer and seller can negotiate who will pay the points on an FHA loan.

Despite the advantage of lower down payments on FHA and VA loans, there are several disadvantages:

- there are limits as to the amounts of these mortgages;

- points increase the costs (the seller could refuse to pay the FHA points); and

- applications are not processed as quickly as they are with conventional fixed rate mortgages.

Adjustable Rate Mortgages (ARMs) offer interest rates which go up and down over the life of the loan as opposed to the conventional fixed rate mortgage. The interest rates of ARMs are tied to one or another of the indices — Treasury securities rate, bank and S & L cost of funds, moving averages of the cost of funds, or even the LIBOR rate (London Interbank offered rate). If you think that interest rates are on their way down, you would prefer your adjustable rate mortgage to be tied to the T-bill index which is much more responsive than the other indices. If the index changes, the variable rate on the mortgage will be adjusted. Thus, monthly mortgage payments will be adjusted upwards when interest rates rise and will decrease when rates go down.

Adjustable rate mortgages became popular when fixed mortgage rates were over 15 percent. ARMs were offered at lower rates than conventional fixed rate mortgages which meant smaller initial monthly payments. However, if mortgage rates rise, you can be hurt by larger monthly payments.

Before accepting an ARM, the following should be considered:

Payment Cap A payment cap protects the borrower by setting the range over which rates can increase or decrease. You should have a cap (of no more than 5 percent) since this limits how high or low your mortgage rate can go. Even a 5-percent cap can make quite a difference in your payments.

Negative Amortization If the rate on an ARM increases significantly but the mortgage payment has a cap, there is the possibility that all the interest expense may not be covered by the mortgage payment. This results in negative amortization. In other words, the mortgage balance would begin to increase instead of decreasing. You should find out if there is a limit on the negative amortization on your ARM. You don't want to have the length of your mortgage increased due to negative amortization.

Frequency of Changes of Mortgage Rates How frequently do the interest rates adjust on an ARM? Some rates change every six months, others are set for a few years and then adjusted for the next few year periods. Try to negotiate the frequency of interest rate changes that are best for you or look for another lender.

The advantages of ARMs are that interest rates tend to be lower than those quoted on conventional mortgages and the interest rate on an ARM goes down when market rates go down.

The disadvantages of ARMs are that the interest rate on an ARM will go up when market rates rise and monthly payments can increase considerably.

Much has been written in the newspapers about the miscalculations many lenders have made on the adjustments to mortgage balances on ARMs. If you have an ARM, check the rates used and monitor your mortgage balances to make sure that you are not being overcharged.

Which Type of Mortgage Should You Choose?

Although only two major types of mortgages, fixed and variable rate, have been discussed, there are many variants of these. No matter what type of mortgage you consider, take the time to understand how the mortgage works and all the intricacies of that mortgage.

In weighing the choices between fixed rate or variable rate mortgages, consider market rates of interest and the length of time you plan to hold the mortgage.

Market Rates of Interest If market rates are low or have been declining over the past few years, you should consider a fixed rate mortgage. Alternatively, if market rates are high, you may be swayed toward a variable rate mortgage. However, if you go with a variable rate mortgage, you should have enough income to be able to cover the monthly payments if the variable rate increases to the maximum limit.

In addition to interest rates, consider the *length of time* you expect to keep the mortgage. If you plan to keep the mortgage for a short while (less than seven years), you could accept an adjustable rate mortgage. However, if you plan to keep the mortgage for a long time, you are better off going with a fixed rate and not having to bear the risks of an increase in interest rates.

What Are the Costs of a Mortgage?

The cost of a mortgage is determined by the interest rate of that mortgage plus any finance charges (points). Interest rates on mortgages fluctuate

110   Chapter 6

over time as well as varying from region to region and are determined by the supply and demand for mortgage funds.

In some cases, financial institutions lower the interest rates on mortgages by 1/4 of a percentage point if you put down a larger down payment. Obviously, the lower the interest rate, the lower the total interest charges on the life of the mortgage. Table 6.6 shows the difference between the monthly payments and total interest charges on a 12 percent, 12.25 percent and 12.5 percent thirty-year loan of $100,000.

Monthly payments can be reduced by roughly $19 every month for each 1/4 percentage point reduction on a $100,000 thirty-year loan. However, the large savings are seen in the total interest expense over the life of the loan, roughly $7,000 less for each 1/4 percentage point reduction on this loan.

Table 6.7 shows a comparison of the monthly payments of thirty-year mortgages ranging from $94,000 to $106,000 at rates ranging from 10.75 percent to 14.25 percent.

By finding the lowest interest rate and putting up a greater down payment, you can reduce your total monthly payments and total interest expense.

Similarly, if you reduce the term of the mortgage from thirty years to fifteen years, the total interest expense paid over the life of the loan will be more than halved as seen in Table 6.8. Monthly payments, however, increase.

Table 6.8, when compared with Table 6.6, illustrates the savings in interest expense with the shorter mortgage.

Several promoters and financial institutions are offering *bi-weekly mortgages*. Instead of paying a mortgage payment once a month, these bi-weekly mortgages require a payment every two weeks. For instance, if your monthly mortgage payment is $1,000, you would, with a bi-weekly mortgage, pay $500 every two weeks which means that you will pay an additional $1,000 every year (twenty-six payments × $500 as opposed to twelve payments × $1,000). You will pay off a thirty-year mortgage in roughly twenty years.

Many of these bi-weekly programs charge fees of $500 to $1,000 for existing mortgage holders to enroll. The second disadvantage is that

---

Table 6.6 $100,000—Thirty-year Mortgage

	12%	12.25%	12.5%
Monthly Payment	$ 1,028.61	$ 1,047.90	$ 1,067.26
Total Interest Expense	$270,308.68	$277,242.72	$284,194.89

Table 6.7

30-Year Monthly Mortgage Payment Comparison Table

%-Rates	94000.00	96000.00	98000.00	100000.00	102000.00	104000.00	106000.00
0.00							
10.75	877.47	896.14	914.81	933.48	952.15	970.82	989.49
11.00	895.18	914.23	933.28	952.32	971.37	990.42	1009.46
11.25	912.99	932.41	951.84	971.26	990.69	1010.11	1029.54
11.50	930.87	950.68	970.49	990.29	1010.10	1029.90	1049.71
11.75	948.85	969.03	989.22	1009.41	1029.60	1049.79	1069.97
12.00	966.90	987.47	1008.04	1028.61	1049.18	1069.76	1090.33
12.25	985.02	1005.98	1026.94	1047.90	1068.85	1089.81	1110.77
12.50	1003.22	1024.57	1045.91	1067.26	1088.60	1109.05	1131.29
12.75	1021.49	1043.23	1064.96	1086.69	1108.43	1130.16	1151.89
13.00	1039.83	1061.95	1084.08	1106.20	1128.32	1150.45	1172.57
13.25	1058.23	1080.74	1103.26	1125.77	1148.29	1170.80	1193.32
13.50	1076.69	1099.60	1122.50	1145.41	1168.32	1191.23	1214.14
13.75	1095.21	1118.51	1141.81	1165.11	1188.41	1211.72	1235.02
14.00	1113.78	1137.48	1161.17	1184.87	1208.57	1232.27	1255.96
14.25	1132.41	1156.50	1180.59	1204.69	1228.78	1252.87	1276.97

112   Chapter 6

Table 6.8 $100,000—Fifteen-year Mortgage

	12%	12.25%	12.5%
Monthly Payment	$ 1,200.17	$ 1,216.30	$ 1,232.78
Total Interest Expense	$116,030.25	$118,933.77	$121,853.97

many promoters will use the money and only submit it to the lending institution on the due date of the regular monthly payment. You lose the time value of your money which could be earning interest for you rather than for a promoter or financial institution.

If you want to reduce the total interest expense of your mortgage and reduce its length, you *don't* need to enroll in a bi-weekly mortgage program. You can do so yourself for no fees (and no cost if there is no prepayment penalty clause in your mortgage) by submitting an extra payment to your mortgage company every year or however many times you would like to pre-pay a portion of your principal. It is a good idea to send a letter with your extra payment to your mortgage company explaining that the amount is to be applied to the principal reduction of your mortgage. When you receive your yearly 1098 mortgage statement for tax purposes, check to see that your mortgage balance has been reduced by the amount of your extra payments.

When to Refinance Your Mortgage

If you have a mortgage which was taken out when interest rates were high and you plan to stay in your present residence for several years, it may pay to refinance your mortgage. To determine whether it is worth refinancing, you have to determine whether the savings from lower interest rates will exceed the costs of refinancing (closing costs which can be 3 percent to 5 percent of the mortgage amount). As a rule of thumb, mortgage rates should come down at least two percentage points for refinancing to be worthwhile. This also applies to adjustable rate mortgage holders who may want to stabilize the amounts of their monthly mortgage payments by locking into a lower fixed rate mortgage.

Bear in mind that points paid to refinance are not fully deductible for federal tax purposes at the time they are paid. Only a portion are deductible each year since the amount is amortized over the life of the mortgage.

How Large a Mortgage Can You Afford?

During the 1980s, lenders were falling over backwards to lend — and this included mortgages and home equity loans. Home equity loans became popular after the Tax Reform Act of 1986 which gradually phased out the tax deductibility of interest on consumer loans. Borrowers of home equity loans, however, could deduct their interest on loans up to $100,000. But with the credit crunch and a possible recession in the early 1990s, the availability of mortgage loans may become tight. The Federal Reserve Bank may keep interest rates low in order to stimulate the economy. Lower interest rates mean that you can afford a larger mortgage. Conversely, of course, a smaller mortgage is more affordable when interest rates are high. It is important to know how large a mortgage you can afford.

As a general rule of thumb, lenders require that payments for housing not exceed about 28 percent of gross income. For instance, if your monthly income is $10,000, your total monthly housing payments — including mortgage, real estate and home insurance — should be no more than $2,800 (28 percent of $10,000). If the real estate taxes on the house are $200 per month and home insurance is $50, the maximum monthly mortgage payment that could be afforded is $2,550 ($2800 – 200 – 50). This is not cast in stone; some lenders may lend more than the 28 percent and some less.

If there are other outstanding debts, such as car loans, cash loans and outstanding credit card balances, lenders may choose not to allow that maximum monthly amount; it may be significantly less. Lenders generally do not want combined debt to exceed 38 percent of gross income (*Business Week*, April 23, 1990, p. 128). By working out how much you can afford for your mortgage payments, you can then determine the maximum amount of your mortgage which then leads you to the range of house prices that you can afford.

Do not overextend yourself with debt because if you cannot make your payments, you could end up losing your assets or find yourself facing personal bankruptcy.

6.3 What to Do if You are Denied Credit

What happens if you apply for credit and get turned down? The first thing to do is ask the creditor why you were turned down.

The Equal Credit Opportunity Act of 1971 requires that the creditor tell you the *specific* reason for your credit rejection. Vague or general reasons are not acceptable. Similarly, in the aftermath of the Equal Credit Opportunity Act of 1975, creditors cannot turn you down because of

114   Chapter 6

your sex or marital status. After 1977, this Act was expanded to make it illegal to deny credit on the basis of age, national origin, race or religion. Creditors must make credit available to all creditworthy customers.

Some reasons for having credit rejected are:

- inadequate or insufficient credit history;

- a history of delinquency;

- not enough income or too much existing debt;

- incomplete credit application;

- poor credit references.

The Fair Credit Reporting Act of 1971, passed to protect consumers from being denied credit due to erroneous or obsolete credit information, assures you of a free look at your credit file (within thirty days of your denial) if you have been denied credit.

By examining your report, you will be able to determine whether your credit information is correct. Reports generally contain credit information for the past year, including the regularity with which you pay your bills (from banks, department stores, utilities, taxes, etc.). This may be coded:

- R1 indicates that you pay your bills on time;

- R2 that you consistently pay bills thirty days late;

- R3 that you consistently pay bills sixty days late; all the way through to,

- R10 which is that you have declared bankruptcy. (*Business Week*, Oct. 2, 1989)

If you find information that is incomplete or erroneous, you may request a reinvestigation. However, if the information pertains to the Internal Revenue Service, the burden of proof falls back to you (*Business Week*, Oct. 2, 1989, p.117).

When a dispute cannot be resolved between you and the credit agency, you have the right to submit your version of the dispute and have it placed in your file.

If you have not been denied credit and want to see the information in your credit file, you can buy a copy ($10-$20) of your credit report from a credit reporting agency. Some of the large agencies are TRW, Equifax, and Trans Union Credit. If you don't know which one has your

Overview of Credit   115

credit file, ask the bank or financial institution where you have a credit card.

6.4   What Are the Alternatives If You Cannot Pay Your Debts?

The loan habit is a difficult one to break. If it started out as one emergency loan which then multiplied to multiple loans, you need to stop and reassess your situation. One more loan may be difficult to get and more costly and this in all likelihood is not going to solve all your problems.

One approach to reassessing your situation is to prepare an income statement, balance sheet and budget. This will give you an accurate picture of your financial condition — whether you have a short-term problem or the other extreme where you are totally engulfed in credit. Your first objective is to make sure that you can make your payments when they are due. If you can service your debt, the next step is to look for ways to start pre-paying your most costly debt. This can come from reducing some unnecessary expenditures or finding ways to augment your income. If you cannot service all your debt payments, you need to decide which debts to pay.

Bank affiliated credit card issuers and nationwide retail credit card issuers generally report to credit bureaus immediately when payments are in default. On the other extreme, bills from professionals, landlords, etc., tend to report to credit bureaus only as a last resort before legal action is taken.

You should be certain to make the highest priority payments first, and then if you can, pay some amounts on all your other debts. It is a good idea to write letters to these creditors explaining that your problems will be rectified within a period of time. However, you should be realistic as to the length of the corrective period. Obviously, if you cannot see an end to your credit problems within a reasonable period of time, you may want to seek outside help.

Serious Overextension

If you cannot devise a repayment plan, you should consider credit counseling. Nonprofit credit counseling offices of the National Foundation for Consumer Credit can be found in most cities. There is a toll-free number. Request a questionnaire; once you have filled it out, you will meet with a credit counselor who will, for a small fee, devise a repayment plan. Counselors will also call or meet with your creditors to get their agreement on the plan. For the plan to work, all of your creditors must agree to the plan and you may be precluded from taking on any new

116   Chapter 6

debt. If the credit counseling office manages your payments to creditors, you will be charged a monthly fee.

For-profit counseling centers (charge much more than their non-profit counterparts) are also available.

Bankruptcy

If you are so swamped with debt that you are unable to take corrective action or if the amounts that you are able to repay are so small that it will take years to pay them off, there is a last resort — personal bankruptcy.

If you choose bankruptcy, you need to decide whether or not to seek legal help. Bankruptcy lawyers may charge a flat fee which would depend on the nature and difficulty of the case. Bankruptcy laws are quite complex and if you do not have a working knowledge of them, it may be advisable to seek legal help. Your lawyer can explain the options of the bankruptcy code and help you to retain more of your assets after filing.

You have two options to choose from within the Bankruptcy Code — Chapter 7, which accounts for the bulk of personal bankruptcy filing — or Chapter 13. Under Chapter 7, a court-appointed trustee takes title to your assets and sells them to raise money to repay creditors. Generally, the proceeds will not cover all of the debts, which means that lenders must settle for less than the amounts that they were owed. The unpaid amounts are cancelled. Certain debts are not exempt and must be fully repaid. You must pay student loans, alimony, child support, unpaid taxes and certain other debts. You may keep certain assets as determined by state laws. Certain states are more generous than others with regard to assets.

Chapter 13 of the Bankruptcy Code allows you, under a court approved plan, to repay debts in part or in full over an extended period of time. This is also known as the *wage earner's plan* because it protects the filer's wages and essential property from being surrendered. Filers pay their debts over the extended period of time but are protected from being sued by their creditors. There are some limitations as to who may file for Chapter 13. Filers may have no more than $350,000 of secured debts and $100,000 of unsecured debts. Similarly, with Chapter 7, there are no guarantees as to the discharges of the debts (*Business Week*, Jan. 21, 1991, p. 91).

Filing for bankruptcy is a last resort and may offer some relief from creditors but there are some major disadvantages. Personal credit records are tainted for a period of ten years, and many people (employers,

Overview of Credit   117

landlords) may view you with disfavor. Finally, bankruptcy is an expensive way to correct the excessive overuse of credit.

Conclusion

Use credit with care and only when necessary. The decade of the 1980s will be referred to as the years of abundant credit. It is expected that the decade of the 1990s will place more emphasis on cash solvency.

CHAPTER 7

AUTOMOBILE AND HOUSING DECISIONS

The largest purchasing decisions most of us make have to do with homes and automobiles. In fact, some automobiles cost more than many houses and they can't even sleep two people! Housing and automobile purchases are relatively expensive and are made infrequently, meaning that time, thought and planning should be expended before purchasing. It can be a costly mistake to purchase an automobile or a house on impulse.

Automobiles

When you have decided that you need an automobile, your thinking may go along the following lines:

- Do I need a new or used car?

- What type of car do I need?

- How will I purchase this car?
  - With cash

  - Finance

  - Lease

7.1 New or Used Automobile?

The decision of whether to buy a new or used car depends primarily on your budget. Used cars may be cheaper to buy than the equivalent new car but maintenance may be higher if the used car is troublesome. Regardless of where you purchase your used car, you should:

- have an idea of the type of car that you would like to buy;

- examine the car thoroughly (particularly the engine, transmission, drive train); and

- be prepared to negotiate the terms and price of the car.

119

120   Chapter 7

Type of Used Car

Before going out to shop for a car, determine the type of car that you need. There are subcompacts, compacts, large cars, station wagons, two-door cars, mini-vans, sports cars and four-wheel-drive cars. Your budget also influences your needs. When you have chosen the type of car, look at the different makes. Do you want an American, European, Japanese or Korean car? Narrow your choices down to a few makes so that you can then compare the terms in your final decision. It is also a good idea to do some research on the maintenance costs and repair records of these models. This information can be found in *Consumer Reports*, *Motor Trend*, *Popular Mechanics* and other auto magazines. You dont want to end up with a model which is a "known lemon" or one that has a costly repair record.

Sources of Used Cars

There are many places to shop for a used car: used car dealers, new car dealers, rental car companies, individuals, auctions of government cars.

Used car dealers sell only used cars and are an excellent source of high mileage, older used cars of different makes. They may even take your existing car as a trade-in on the purchase of a used car. However, because used car dealers do not have service departments, they offer very limited warranties on their cars. You can often negotiate a lower price from a used car dealer than from other sources on the same model.

New car dealers have service departments and the warranties may be more extensive than those offered by used car dealers. Disadvantages are that car prices tend to be higher at new car dealers and the cross section of different models may not be as extensive.

Rental car companies often sell their cars after they are one or two years old. You can ask to see the maintenance records on the car you are interested in. Many rental companies give service contracts and since they are late model cars, they may still be under warranty from the manufacturer.

Individuals or private owners also sell their cars and are a good source for older cars. However, such cars do not come with warranties (unless they are late models which are still warranted by the manufacturer). You buy the car "as is" which is why you should be very careful when buying a car through a private owner. Ask about the maintenance and repairs on the car and whether you can see the receipts of those repairs.

Examine the Car

No matter where you buy your used car, you should examine it thoroughly. Inspect all the physical features. Test drive the car on the highway to see how it performs at faster speeds. Look for fluid leaks. If you are satisfied with the car, have a mechanic whom you trust examine the mechanical workings of the car. If repairs or potential repairs are indicated, get estimates of the costs in writing.

Journalists have reported many scams including those involving certain used car dealers who have sold cars which were immaculate in exterior appearance but so mechanically unsound that they broke down after a short time. Owners who had financed these cars stopped making the payments to the financial institutions because the cars required such costly repairs. The financial institutions then repossessed these cars and auctioned them off at very low prices which did not cover the amount of the loans. The buyers of the used cars then found that they still owed money on the loans of their repossessed cars. The courts then forced the buyers to pay their debts in full.

If you don't check the mechanical soundness of a used car before buying it, you run the risk of buying someone else's repair costs.

Negotiate

Many people, when they are ready to buy, take out their checkbooks and write a check for the asking price. There is nothing wrong with this approach if you know that the asking price is a "fair" price. Most sellers inflate their asking price and almost expect to be negotiated down. You can determine the fair price of a used car from various publications such as *Edmund's Used Car Prices* or the *Official Used Car Guide* (also known as "the blue book"). These can be found at bookstores, libraries, banks and financial institutions. The blue book quotes apply to cars which are in good condition and have relatively low mileage for their age. Other guides may quote different prices for the same model such as the retail value, wholesale value and the loan value. *Retail value* is what a car dealer would sell the car for; *wholesale value* is what a dealer would pay for the car and *loan value* is what a lender would lend to a purchaser to finance the car.

Always offer the seller less than the asking price which should be below the retail value if the auto is in excellent condition, has no potential repair bills looming and relatively low mileage for its age. If there are some things wrong with the car which need to be repaired, deduct these

122   Chapter 7

costs from the asking price and offer a lower price. The buyer has everything to gain by trying to bargain the seller (all sources of sellers) down from the asking price.

New Car

If you set out to look for a used car, you may discover that for a little more money up front, you can buy a new car. When deciding to buy a new car, the first step is to determine the amount that you can spend. The most obvious cost is the purchase price but there are also operating and maintenance costs down the road. The next step is to consider which type and model of car you are interested in.

7.2   What Type of Car?

Some say "a car is a car is a car." It has four wheels and gets you from one destination to another. Others disagree and feel that one make of car is distinctly different from another. Not only do cars vary in size, shape and form, many come with different options and perform differently. In making your decisions, you need to identify the model and type of car that is best for you. There are subcompacts, compacts, intermediates and full-size-cars, as well as American, European, Japanese and Korean cars to choose from.

Within the categories of car sizes are different styles of cars; you also need to look at the features of the cars you consider.

Some makes of cars include certain optional equipment as part of their standard price, so it becomes important to compare the features of the different models offered by the different car manufacturers.

There are also safety features that you may want to consider when making your decision. Many cars have driver side air bags and some of the larger cars have dual air bags: anti-lock brakes, traction control and a reinforced steel cage with crumple zones are other important safety features. Knowing your needs can help you (and your pocketbook) in your final decision.

7.3   How to Purchase a Car

When you have narrowed your decision to the type, style, features and brands of cars that you are interested in, you should do some more investigating before you encounter a salesman in the showroom.

Make a list of the models that you are interested in and visit the dealer's lots on a Sunday or in the evening when you can look at the cars without any sales pressure. List the standard features and the suggested sales prices (the list prices) which you can read from the stickers pasted on the windows of the new cars.

Your next step is to find out the dealer's cost for each of the cars, because the dealer's costs can vary from 10 percent to 25 percent below the list price. The annual *Kelley Blue Book New Car Price Manual* and *Edmund's New Car Prices* list the dealer's cost for all new models. Another source of the dealer's cost is the April *Consumer Reports* magazine. Armed with this information, you are in a better negotiating position. In addition to dealer's cost, you want to know how reliable the cars on your list are. The April *Consumer Reports* rates the different cars in the marketplace in terms of their repair and maintenance costs, based on the results of owner surveys. Most consumer automotive magazines such as *Car and Driver, Road and Track, Motor Trend* and *Popular Mechanics* feature tests and reports on different new cars in each of their issues. If there is a favorable review, you are bound to see it in the dealer's showroom. However, you will want to rule out buying a car which has known flaws and one that will end up spending more time in the dealer's garage than your own.

You should also study these car magazines to see if any model changes loom in the near future. So often people will buy a model paying close to list price only to find a new model coming out in the next few months that will replace their existing model. Salespeople may not be forthcoming with this information if they are not asked and some may not even be aware of the impending model change.

Another factor to consider is the time of year that you buy the car. Most new models come out in September and October for the next year but some carmakers bring out their new models at other times of the year to get an edge on their competition. If you are buying a model toward the end of the model year, you should negotiate a substantial discount since new cars depreciate the most in their first years.

You are now "armed and ready" to visit the dealers. Test drive the cars you are interested in to narrow down your choices. When you have decided on a model, negotiate with the salesperson. The salesperson's delight is the person who takes out a checkbook and writes the check for the sticker (list) price. Ask the salesperson for the best price and then proceed to bargain.

If the price that the salesperson quotes is still too high or if it is still very close to list price, visit another dealer who sells the same make of car. In fact, you should never buy a car from the first dealer you visit. Check the competition and then go back to the closest dealer, the one with the best service department or the one with the lowest price, to see

124   Chapter 7

whether they can do any better to get your business. Selling can be a game and if you play the game you will get a fairer price.

I know a couple who "played the game" so effectively that the owner of the dealership took them up to his office to show them the cost on the invoice from the manufacturer to prove why he could not go down any further in price.

If you have a trade-in, you need to establish the retail and wholesale value of the car, in order to determine what price would be acceptable. First, negotiate the price of the new car before you mention the trade-in. Why work hard to get a good discount on the new car only to *capitulate* by selling your trade-in at a *give away* price? If you do not get a fair price, you could sell your car privately or visit another dealer. Many people prefer to trade their cars in rather than go through the trouble of selling their cars privately. Another advantage of trading your car in on the purchase is that you reduce the amount of the sales taxes that you have to pay. For example, if the new car price that you negotiate is $10,000 and you accept $4,000 on your trade-in, you pay state sales taxes only on the difference of $6,000, not on the full $10,000. If the state sales tax is 6 percent, this would result in a $240 saving ($360 versus $600). If you sold your car privately, state taxes would be assessed on the full purchase price of $10,000.

It is extremely important to know what figures you are aiming for in your negotiations particularly when you are trading a car in on the purchase. After you have negotiated your deal, you can determine how to pay for the purchase — cash, finance or lease.

Should You Pay Cash?

If you have the money and special low-rate loans are not available from the automobile manufacturing companies, pay cash. For instance, Saab Scania offered attractive financing rates of 2.15 percent per annum (p.a.). on the purchase price of a Saab 900 model and 4.35 percent p.a. on a Saab 9000 for four years. In this case, it would be advantageous to finance the purchase and invest your cash in a certificate of deposit paying 7 percent p.a.

Should You Finance?

Since automobiles are expensive, many people choose to finance their purchases. Even though you may decide at the outset to finance, you should still go through the negotiation process to obtain the best price on a car in order to achieve lower payments. Car loans are available

Automobiles and Housing Decisions   125

from several sources, banks, credit unions, dealer financing and other financial institutions as discussed in Chapter 6.

Ask the dealer if there are any subsidized low-rate interest loans available from the automobile manufacturer. Even if the rate of interest is lower than competitive rates, you need to make sure that the loan amount is based on your negotiated price and not the list price. Often manufacturers will offer low interest rate loans of zero percent, 1 percent etc. but they will inflate the price to get back part of their subsidy.

Car manufacturers have also offered rebates instead of low rate subsidized loans (often where the car price is inflated to the list price). In certain cases, it may be better to take the rebates which will lower the purchase price and then find your own financing from banks, credit unions etc.

When comparing different sources of financing, check the APRs which represent the true cost of the loan. For example, the loan with the lowest monthly payments may not necessarily have the lowest cost because you may be paying the payments for a longer period of time and the finance charges may be much greater.

When you take out financing, do not buy life or disability insurance in conjunction with the loan. These premiums are expensive and you do not need them. If you are underinsured, you are better off looking at your needs independently of your purchase.

Should You Lease your Automobile?

Automobile leasing has become extremely popular. This is evident in the newspapers where more and more automotive advertisements contain information about leasing. Just because leasing has become very popular, however, does not mean that it's the right alternative for you.

There are two basic types of leases: open-ended and closed-ended. An *open-end lease* involves monthly lease payments made for the period of the lease. At the end of the lease, a final payment — based on the resale value of the car — is made to buy the car. With a *closed-end lease*, lease payments are made over the lease period. At the end of the lease, you hand in the keys and walk away from the car. Certain conditions apply such as returning the car in a reasonable condition and not exceeding the maximum mileage set by the leasing company.

Most of the advertisements in the newspapers are for closed-end leases and ads often claim or imply that leasing is cheaper than financing or buying. Don't be misled — leasing companies have to buy the cars that they lease and after the lease period these cars have depreciated considerably. Consequently, leasing companies charge to recover both the interest costs that they have paid out for buying the cars and the

126   Chapter 7

amount of the depreciation of the cars (the fall in resale value when the car is returned to them), their overhead and a certain amount of profit.

In a closed-end lease, it is important to ask what rate of interest the leasing company uses and whether the automobile that you have selected has a low or high resale value. These two factors will determine the amount of the lease payments.

Leasing a car often turns out to be more costly than financing a car, even though the monthly payments on a closed-end lease are less than the monthly payments to finance the car. In a closed-end lease, you have "rented" the car for the lease period. If you were to buy the car and finance the purchase, you would pay the entire purchase price plus the interest expense. However, if you keep the car in relatively good condition, you can sell the car at the end of the same period and the net outlay for financing generally will be less than the net outlay for leasing (closed-end).

An open-end lease works the same way as financing the car but the terms can be structured in such a way that it becomes more costly than straight financing. When leasing a car, many people assume that they cannot negotiate the purchase price. By accepting the higher list price put forward by the leasing company, your lease payments will be higher than if you negotiated a lower price and then based the lease on that lower price. What is often overlooked in an open-end lease is that the residual value (the amount of the payment at the end of the lease to buy the car) can be flexible. In other words, if the residual value is increased, the monthly lease payments will be lower. Similarly, the residual payment can be as low as $1, which means that the monthly lease payments will be higher.

Be aware of the fine print in the lease agreements which will include the extra charges for excess mileage, the amount of the down payment, etc. You should negotiate these items: increase the mileage limits if there is a possibility that you will exceed them and try to avoid having to make a down payment.

Leasing may be advantageous for the following reasons:

- If you do not have enough cash either to buy a car or for a down payment in financing, leasing becomes attractive since it requires either no down payment or a small down payment.

- Monthly lease payments may be less than the monthly payments for financing.

- You are not tying up your money in a car. You can invest the funds that you would have used as a down payment for financing (or buying).

Automobiles and Housing Decisions   127

- If you like to change cars every few years and you always finance them, you may be better off leasing them. If you keep your car longer than five years, you should not lease.

To summarize, it is generally cheaper to buy a car by paying cash, second cheapest to finance and leasing comes last. In all transactions, read through the sales contract before signing and always check the figures.

Housing

Housing decisions are extremely important from many viewpoints. The purchase of a home is probably the largest single expenditure of funds that individuals make. For renters, rental expenses could account for up to 40 percent of their monthly budgets. However, the housing decision goes beyond financial expenditures because where you choose to live will determine your commuting time to work, access to shopping, your neighborhood friends, your children's friends, the school system etc.. A tremendous amount of time and thought are invested in making housing decisions.

Housing decisions involve two basic alternatives: renting or buying. Most people in America own homes but the median price of new homes has been increasing virtually every year making home ownership unaffordable for many people, particularly young families just starting out. People who can't afford to buy end up renting.

7.4   Renting Decisions

In addition to financial reasons, people rent because they may not want to be faced with the responsibilities of home ownership or they may expect to be in a location temporarily. Renters are faced with several choices: they could rent apartments, townhouses or individual homes.

The type of accommodations chosen will depend on the renter's circumstances and needs for space.

Rental Agreement Renters are usually required to sign a rental agreement which contains the provisions of the rental. This is a legally binding document and renters should read and understand all the provisions before signing it. Some of the key points are:

- The amount of the rent, the due date and the frequency of payments.

- The amount of the security deposit that the renter may be required to leave with the landlord (which varies between one

128   Chapter 7

and three months rent) and the conditions for the return of the security deposit at the end of the lease. The security deposit is returned if the premises are left in relatively good condition. If there are to be any charges against the deposit, these conditions should be clearly and explicitly stated in the agreement. Examine the premises very carefully for any damage before you move in, document any existing damage in writing and have this signed by the landlord. In certain states, landlords are required to pay interest on the security deposit.

- Who will be responsible for paying for utilities, insurance, repairs, maintenance, garbage collection, real estate taxes, and other expenses? These should be clearly spelled out; if you have any doubts, clarify them before you sign the agreement.

- The rental period, conditions to renew the lease, how the rental increases will be determined and the conditions for early termination must be clearly stated in the lease. If there is no escape clause, include one which states that if there are any mitigating circumstances you can break your lease by paying one-month's rent.

- Restrictions, if any, on the use of the property are listed. These could apply to pets, children, noise, alterations to the premises, subletting, numbers of occupants, etc.

If you succeed in negotiating any waivers to the conditions set out in the contract, they should be documented in writing, attached to the contract and signed by the landlord.

There are several advantages to renting:

- You have greater mobility when you rent. When your lease expires, you can leave without having to sell the property. If mobility is important to you, do not tie yourself down with a long-term lease without an escape clause.

- You are not tying up your money (other than the amount of the security deposit) which means that you can invest this money or use it for other purposes.

- Renting may require reduced expenses toward maintenance and repairs. Landlords are usually responsible for most, if not all, of the repairs.

The disadvantages of renting are:

Automobiles and Housing Decisions   129

- Your rental payments give you no ownership interests.

- You have no control over rental increases.

- If the property appreciates, you do not share in the appreciation.

- You cannot deduct your rental payments against your federal taxes (interest on a mortgage and real estate taxes are currently tax-deductible expenses).

- You may be restricted by your lease from having pets or starting a family.

- You could have noisy, inconsiderate neighbors or an ineffectual landlord.

7.5   Home Ownership

Renting a house is much simpler and less time consuming than buying a house. For example, if you rent a house in a neighborhood which has poor schools or high crime, you can easily move out. If you had bought the house, the solution would be more time consuming to rectify and probably more costly.

In buying a house, you need to define your needs and rank them in terms of importance. For example, do you want to be in the city, in the suburbs, near a shopping center, within walking distance of public transportation, near a playground, in a neighborhood with a strong school system, etc.?

Many real estate brokers will tell you that the *location* is more important than the house. For example, a large, well built, well maintained house behind a highway or on a busy street or in a deteriorating neighborhood, may not appreciate in price. In fact, it may depreciate and cost less than a smaller home in a better neighborhood. However, when it comes to selling the house in a poor location, not only could you lose money, it may not sell easily or quickly.

In addition to a good location, you should evaluate prices of surrounding homes in that area. You do not want to end up buying the most expensive house in the neighborhood because the values of properties around your house will have an influence as to the amount of appreciation. For example, if you buy a $200,000 house in a neighborhood surrounded by $100,000 homes, it will not appreciate as much as it would in a neighborhood with other $200,000 homes.

You should check to see that the properties surrounding your home are zoned for residential use. You don't want to end up with neighbors

130   Chapter 7

consisting of stores, gas stations and companies. You may also want to find out whether the zoning includes multifamily homes. Checking the zoning is particularly important if your prospective house abuts a vacant property.

The next question to consider is how much can you afford to spend on the house that will satisfy your needs. Two rough guidelines apply to the affordability of a home:

- All housing expenditures (including mortgage, real estate taxes and insurance) should be less than ±28 percent of your gross income; and

- The house price can equal roughly 2 1/4 to 2 1/2 times your annual income.

However, these quick and easy formulas may be inaccurate for a large percentage of cases because everyone's financial circumstances are different. You need to consider many additional factors such as, do you have enough cash for the down payment and closing costs, can you maintain the house, etc.?

If you finance your house, lenders require that you put some equity into the purchase, which is a *down payment.* Minimum down payments can vary from 5 percent to 20 percent of the purchase price. For instance, a $100,000 house may be unaffordable if the lender requires a 20-percent down payment ($20,000) as opposed to a 5-percent down payment ($5,000) for someone whose income will qualify for a $95,000 mortgage but who does not have $20,000 in cash.

You'll also need to have enough cash to cover the mortgage points and closing costs. *Mortgage points* are up-front fees which lenders charge for borrowing. These vary from 1 percent to 3 percent of the mortgage loan. Hence, two mortgage points on a $95,000 mortgage would cost the buyer $1,900 (2 percent × $95,000). If the points are paid up-front with a separate check at settlement, they are fully tax deductible in the year that you buy the house. However, if the points are in the form of origination fees, they are only deductible when the house is sold for a profit. Always check with your accountant because there have been many changes in the Tax Code and this treatment may have changed by the time you are ready to purchase your house.

Closing Costs are the costs of settlement which can average between 3 percent and 6 percent of the cost of the house. These include the costs for a title search, title insurance, attorneys' fees and recording fees.

Even if you have enough cash to cover the down payment, mortgage points and closing costs, you need to be able to cover the costs of owning the house. These would include your monthly mortgage payments, real estate taxes, home insurance premiums, utility costs, maintenance and repairs. You need to consider whether you can cover increases in any of these costs. The most accurate determination of how much you can afford to spend on a house is to compile a budget. You can then translate this amount into the maximum mortgage that you can afford. Determine this by looking at mortgage tables (sold in most bookstores).

There are *several types* of houses that are available for purchase. The most common are: mobile homes, condominiums and conventional homes.

From a homeowner's point of view, there are many advantages to ownership:

- Over long periods of time, most housing units appreciate in value and prices tend to keep pace with inflation. Home ownership could be considered an investment in a sense, as well as a hedge against inflation.

- Home ownership provides some tax relief in that the interest expense on the mortgage and the real estate taxes are deductible items from taxable income at the federal level. Interest expense on a mortgage is not subject to being added back in the computation of the alternative minimum tax (AMT).

- Over time, homeowners increase their equity position in their homes if they had financed their purchase. A portion of each mortgage payment goes toward the repayment of the mortgage. Thus, over time, homeowners owe less and their equity stake increases.

- Homeowners who have sufficient equity in their homes or who have seen price appreciation of their homes, can use this build-up as a source of providing new loans—home equity loans, for example.

- If a homeowner sells a home for a profit and buys another house for at least the sales price or a greater amount within two years of the sale, capital gains can be deferred.

- Home ownership provides more freedom than renting. There are no landlords and no restrictions concerning pets, children, etc.

132   Chapter 7

- Home ownership often brings about a greater personal commitment to the neighborhood and community activities.

The disadvantages of homeownership are:

- With ownership, you bear the financial risks if any events cause property values to fall. If you have to sell when the property market is down, you could lose money.

- Home ownership decreases your mobility. It may not be that easy to sell a house and move to another location in a short period of time.

7.6   Should You Rent or Buy?

The question of whether to rent or buy is a matter of individual choice. It is relatively easy to list the financial factors concerning renting and buying but the nonfinancial considerations are much more difficult to weigh.

The financial factors to consider involve comparing the costs of renting with the costs of buying to see which would be lower. See Table 7.1 for a comparison of these costs. The calculation in this example is used only to illustrate the process involved and is not meant to show that it is always less costly to buy. In some areas, rental expenses may be very low and interest rates on mortgages may be comparatively high, making the mortgage payments very high. Consequently, it may be beneficial to rent until mortgage interest rates come down. The 15-percent to 17-percent mortgage interest rates in the early part of 1980 stalled many would-be house buyers.

In the example, in Table 7.1, it is more costly to rent than the after tax costs of buying ($14,042 versus $12,414). You also need to consider that many of these figures will change over a period of a few years: rent increases, increased home maintenance costs, decreasing mortgage interest expenses and possible short-term appreciation/depreciation of home prices. Home ownership provides many more financial advantages.

If you intend to move in the near future, renting may be more advantageous than buying. However, this would not have been true during the housing boom of the late 1970s and early 1980s when house prices increased significantly over short periods of time.

The decision of whether to rent or buy is not always clear-cut or easy. An evaluation of both the financial and nonfinancial aspects helps to resolve the dilemma.

7.7 Guidelines for Buying a Home

- Select the town, area or location where you want to live.

- Select a real estate broker — generally this will save you time and effort. By looking through the Multiple Listing Service directory in a broker's office you can see the houses of interest and eliminate the others. Realtors are paid commissions by the sellers so their interests lie with the seller of the property. Remember, realtors get paid only when there is a sale and the buyer's interests may be secondary.

- Look at several houses and narrow them down to the few that fulfill your requirements. By looking at many houses you will get a feeling for house prices in the area. If you are interested in an older house, examine the overall condition very critically. If it requires major repairs (for example, a new roof, new plumbing, replacing windows) call a contractor for estimates. Don't rely on the broker's guesses. Deduct these estimates from the price that you think is a fair price to offer. Don't be influenced by the broker to increase the price above the amount that you think is a fair price. If you are considering a new house that is being built, investigate the builder's financial soundness and whether there are any complaints lodged against the builder. (This information can be obtained from the Better Business Bureau, the Attorney General's Office and the Department of Consumer Protection). Visit some of the homes that the builder has completed and ask the owners if they are satisfied with the quality of the construction.

- After your offer price has been accepted, the broker will present you with a sales agreement. If you are going to use a lawyer, this is the time to get the lawyer involved. Most sales agreements use a standard format and a lawyer may choose to rewrite the contract or add certain clauses for the buyer's protection. If you are not using a lawyer, make sure that the agreement has the following conditions:

  - the agreement of sale is subject to a favorable building inspection. You want an escape clause if an inspector finds that the house is infested with termites, or is structurally unsound, or that you need to break through walls to repair

134   Chapter 7

Table 7.1 Comparison of the Costs of Renting versus Buying a Home Annual Cost of Renting

Annual Cost of Renting

Rent	$1,000 × 12	$12,000
Utilities	150 × 12	1,800
Tenant's Insurance		200
Interest Foregone on the the deposit		
$1,000 × 6% × 30% marginaltax rate*)		42
Total Annual Cost of Renting		$14,042

Annual Cost of Buying with a Mortgage of $90,000 at 10%

Mortgage Payments	$967 × 12	$11,604
Real Estate Taxes		2,400
Maintenance and Repairs	100 × 12	1,200
Utilities	200 × 12	2,400
Insurance		500
Interest Foregone on the the deposit		
$10,000 × 6% × 30% marginal tax rate*)		420
Gross Annual Cost		18,524

Less Tax Savings from Deductions:		
Interest on Mortgage	$8,877	
Real Estate Taxes	2,400	
	11,277	
× by the marginal Tax Rate ×	30%	
Tax Savings		(3,383)
		$15,524
Less Equity Build-up		(2,727)
Net Annual Cost of Buying		$12,414

These costs could be adjusted further
for any appreciation of the property.

* A 30% marginal tax rate is assumed.

Automobiles and Housing Decisions   135

leaking pipes. Should any major defects be found and you still want the house, you should either renegotiate the price, or have the seller pay for the repairs. You should also get your own building inspector and not rely on the broker's list of available inspectors. I know of a case where the inspector was "bought off" by the broker and ignored several major defects in the house.

— the agreement of sale is subject to the buyer obtaining a mortgage at favorable or competitive rates of interest.

— the interest on the escrowed deposit is paid to the buyer.

— the right to inspect the property before settlement takes place. This is when you would note that everything is in the condition you expect it to be, and if the seller has made the repairs expected. If the seller is not in compliance or the property has been damaged, an amount of money should be held back in escrow with your attorney at settlement until there is full compliance.

— the house and garden are in good repair, well maintained and clean.

Read through the agreement carefully before you sign it. Buying a house is one of the largest purchases you will make, so take your time at each stage and don't allow anyone to pressure you or rush you into something you may regret.

7.8   Second Homes

Many Americans dream of second homes or vacation homes such as a shore house, a cottage at a lake, a country home or a condominium at the seashore or in the mountains. Many different reasons motivate the purchase of a second home. Second homes may be purchased purely for their enjoyment and the possibility of future capital gains or, at the other extreme, purely as an investment property which will be rented out.

As we saw in the previous section, homeownership provides the possibility of capital appreciation, tax benefits and an additional benefit of being able to defer profits in certain situations.

Personal Use

If you use your second home personally and do not rent it out for more than fourteen days or 10 percent of the time that you use it, the Internal

136   Chapter 7

Revenue Service considers it to be your personal residence. Tax laws keep changing but currently you can deduct the interest expense and real estate taxes on two personal residences. There are restrictions as to the total amount of interest that can be deducted and the deductible interest is only for the loans up to the price paid for the house (or houses) plus the value of certain improvements. Maintenance costs and depreciation are not tax-deductible expenses for federal tax purposes.

In addition to capital appreciation, real estate tends to be an excellent hedge against inflation. During periods of high inflation in the late 1970s and early 1980s, property prices kept pace with rates of inflation.

If you sell your principal residence, you can defer the gains made on the sale by buying another house that costs the same or more than the selling price of your old house, within a period of two years.

As a Rental Property

If you rent your home out for more than fourteen days a year or more than 10 percent of the time that you use it, it is classified as a rental property. The Tax Reform Act of 1986 took away many of the tax advantages of rental properties. If the property was purchased after 1986, the depreciation period is longer (27 1/2 years for residential property and 31 1/2 years for commercial property) which means that depreciation expenses will be smaller.

If the property produces losses, these losses are considered "passive" losses. This means that you can only deduct up to $25,000 of the losses against your income, if you provide active management of the property and your adjusted gross income is less than $100,000 for a married person filing jointly or $50,000 for a married person filing separately. This loss allowance gets phased out as adjusted gross income reaches $150,000 (or $75,000 for married couples filing separately). When adjusted gross income exceeds $150,000, no losses can be deducted against your income but there are still some cash flow benefits. You may still come out ahead if your rental income covers some of your expenses such as maintenance and repairs, insurance and depreciation. You should keep an account of the losses which can be offset when you sell the rental property. Invest in rental property where the rental income is greater than your costs.

In some cases, when adjusted gross income exceeds $150,000, it may be more beneficial financially to convert the rental property to a personal residence where mortgage interest expenses and real estate taxes can be deducted from income. Thus, when buying a second house for rental income, consult your accountant first to see where you stand in terms of tax benefits.

Automobiles and Housing Decisions   137

Overall, there are many advantages and disadvantages to second homes. Disadvantages include:

- Maintenance and repairs may be high, particularly if you have destructive tenants.

- Homes that remain unoccupied for long periods of time may fall prey to vandalism.

- Second homes may not be easy to sell — particularly in down markets — and, therefore, tend to be illiquid investments.

- There are tax disadvantages due to the changes in the Tax Reform Act of 1986 which need to be weighed against the advantages of:

  - The possibility of capital gains in the future;
  - The income potential; and
  - The pure enjoyment of a second home.

7.9 Time-Sharing

Time-sharing has become popular in certain parts of the country. Developers of condominiums sell time shares in the condominium which give purchasers the right to use a unit for a period of time every year. The time span varies from one to four week periods. If you do not want to go back to the same place every year, you can swap your right for someone else's right in another place. The range of venues offered depends on where you buy your time-sharing.

Time shares can be resold but they have tended to not appreciate as much as traditional real estate. In fact, ownership in time-sharing properties is so diffuse that owners have very little control over anything concerning the management, maintenance, etc. It tends to be a limiting experience and many time-share owners in the past have fallen victim to abusive business practices of unscrupulous promoters and developers. Time-sharing should be bought for vacation purposes and not as an investment.

APPENDIX

How to Invest

Investment basics were presented in the preceding chapters. This section contains an overview of the various types of investment instruments, beginning with the savings account, the most common form of personal investment. Other investment types are arranged in alphabetic order:

1. Safe Haven Savings Instruments
2. Bonds:
   Corporate Bonds
   Government Agency Bonds
   Junk Bonds
   Municipal Bonds
   Treasury Bonds & Notes
   Zero-Coupon Bonds
3. Closed-end Funds
4. Common Stocks
5. Convertible Securities
6. Mutual Funds
7. Preferred Stock
8. Treasury Bills
9. U.S. Savings Bonds

This list includes some of the more popular investments but is by no means complete. Certain investment instruments may not be suitable due to their risks, time horizons, lack of liquidity and/or marketability. To diversify risks, increase the types of investments you make to include more than just savings accounts, certificates of deposit and common stock.

1   SAFE HAVEN SAVINGS INSTRUMENTS

There are many different types of savings accounts offered by banks, savings & loan associations and credit unions. Savings accounts and certificates of deposit (CDs) are often referred to as *safe havens* for money because you get back the amount you invest. It is wise to keep

139

140   Appendix

a certain amount of money (depending on your liquidity needs) in such risk-free accounts. That does not mean that all of your money should be put into these accounts — the amount you put into such accounts will depend on your cash needs.

Checking Accounts are the most liquid of all accounts offered by banks and savings and loan institutions because checks are payable on demand. Traditional checking accounts earn no interest and have no minimum balance. Money that you do not need should not be left idle in checking accounts. It's a bit like storing money under your mattress — you are not earning a return. (Even checking accounts, however, have an advantage over the "mattress" in that they are insured by a government agency.)

Negotiated Order of Withdrawal (NOW) Accounts With bank deregulation in the early 1980s came NOW accounts — checking accounts which pay low rates of interest and have minimum balances. If your balance falls below the minimum required by the institution, you may not earn interest on the balance in the account and you may be subjected to additional bank charges.

Super NOW Accounts and Money Market Checking Accounts generally pay higher rates of interest than NOW accounts and require larger minimum balances. At many institutions, if a balance falls below the minimum amount, the Super NOW would revert to a NOW account. Service charges and fees vary among different institutions; you should shop around to compare interest rates, minimum balances and service charges.

Non-Certificate Savings Accounts are offered by banks, thrift institutions and credit unions and offer the lowest interest rates. They are designed for people who have small amounts of money to invest. Amounts deposited in such accounts can be withdrawn without advance notice to the institution.

Money Market Deposit Accounts came into existence in the 1970s, and savers quickly took their money out of low-yielding savings accounts and put them into the higher yielding money market deposit accounts. Money market deposit accounts require minimum balances, offer liquidity and pay money market interest rates which are slightly lower than those offered by money market mutual funds and Treasury bills (T-bills).

Interest rates change daily or weekly as the nation's money supply fluctuates. There are also variations in the rates that banking institutions will pay. Take the time to shop around to find the institution with the highest effective yield.

Certificates of Deposit (CDs) are issued by banking institutions in various amounts (the minimum range can be from $500 to $5,000) and

How to Invest   141

variable maturities (seven days to thirty months). The depositor receives a certificate as a receipt for the funds deposited for the specified period of time.

Life would be simple if banks all paid the same rate of interest for CDs of the same maturity but both interest rates and frequency of interest payments vary. When comparing CDs from different institutions, be sure to choose the CD which pays the highest effective yield. If you have large amounts to invest ($50,000 to $100,000 and more), a higher rate of interest can often be negotiated at many banking institutions. Be aware, however, that there are early withdrawal penalties for most if not all CDs if you withdraw your money before the maturity date.

HOW TO BUY

Checking and deposit accounts can be opened at banks, thrifts (Savings & Loan Associations) and credit unions. CDs are offered by banks, thrifts and brokerage firms.

Accounts at banks and thrifts are currently insured by the Federal Deposit Insurance Corporation (FDIC) and Federal Savings and Loan Insurance Corporation (FSLIC) respectively for amounts up to $100,000 per individual per institution. These insurance limits could change due to the bailouts of some savings and loans and banks by the FSLIC and FDIC. If limits stay as they are, a married couple could have insurance of up to $300,000 at the same institution by opening up accounts (including CDs) in the husband's name for $100,000, accounts in the wife's name up to $100,000 and joint accounts up to $100,000. If you have more than $300,000, you could increase your insurance protection by opening up accounts at different banks and thrifts.

Be wary of opening accounts or investing in "junk" CDs (which are subordinated notes) not insured by the FDIC or FSLIC. Check that your brokered CDs are issued by institutions that have FDIC or FSLIC insurance. By having your deposits and CDs insured by federal agencies, you have virtually eliminated the risk of loss of principal and interest.

ADVANTAGES

- With Federal agency insurance checking, deposit accounts and CDs are very safe investments. The difference in the rates offered by uninsured institutions is so small that it is not worth risking the loss of your savings by investing in the accounts of uninsured institutions.

142   Appendix

- These accounts offer the growth of principal through interest being compounded. CDs offer higher rates of interest than deposit and checking accounts.

- Checking and some deposit accounts offer immediate liquidity whereas longer maturity CDs are less liquid. The maturity of CDs can be staggered so as not to mature at the same time, allowing some flexibility.

- CDs marketed by brokers and traders have a secondary market (they can be bought and sold before maturity at market prices which will rise and fall depending on the prevailing market rates of interest).

DISADVANTAGES

- Savings accounts and CDs offer little protection against inflation since interest rates may not rise significantly to cover rising rates of inflation.

- Interest is taxed by all levels of government (federal, state and/or local).

- There are no capital gains (or loss) opportunities on any of these accounts except for brokered CDs which are traded on secondary markets.

- If you need to sell a bank CD before maturity, there is a withdrawal penalty. Some institutions, in fact, may not allow early withdrawal except in cases of severe hardship.

- Brokered CDs traded on the secondary markets are exposed to interest rate risks. For example, a brokered CD issued at 8 percent would trade at a discount before maturity if market rates of interest went up to 9 percent.

CAVEATS

- Do not park large amounts of money in noninterest-bearing checking accounts. Instead, keep these funds in money market accounts and transfer the funds to your checking account when they are needed.

- Shop around for the banking institution with the best terms (effective interest rate, early withdrawal penalties and minimum balances) before investing.

- Check to see if the interest on your CD earns compound interest. If not, have the financial institution deposit the interest automatically into a money market account.

- Compare CD rates offered by local banks with the Bankquote Deposit Index listed in the Friday edition of the *Wall Street Journal*, before tying up your funds.

CONCLUSION

Federally insured savings accounts and shorter term CDs provide savers a low risk place to invest funds which may be needed on short notice. (See also Treasury bills and money market mutual funds for alternative investments of short-term funds.)

2 BONDS
CORPORATE BONDS

DEFINITION

A *corporate bond* is a loan made by the bondholder to a corporation (which issues the bond). The corporation pays a specified rate of interest and repays the face value of the bond at a specified maturity date. The interest (coupon) rate is generally fixed for the life of the bond. The face (par) value of most bonds is usually $1,000 (there are some bonds with a face value of $500). Thus, a bond with a coupon rate of 8 percent would pay interest of $80 per year (8 percent of $1,000 face value).

Bonds are sensitive to market interest rates and do not necessarily sell at their face value. They may trade at discounts (less than $1,000), face value, or premiums (over $1,000) depending on the market rate of interest in relation to the coupon rate of the bond. When market rates of interest rise above the coupon rate of the bond, the bond price will decline in order to relate the coupon rate to the market rate. When interest rates fall, the price of the bond will rise. Vulnerable to interest rates, bond prices vary with the length of time to maturity. Shorter term bonds are

144   Appendix

less sensitive to interest rate fluctuations, while longer term bond prices will be more volatile due to changing interest rates.

Corporate bonds are rated by appraisal services such as Moody's Investor Services and Standard & Poor's Bond Guide as to the credit-worthiness of the issuing corporation, the likelihood of default on interest and principal, the type of protection for the bondholder in the event of bankruptcy and the investment quality of the issue. Moody's and Standard & Poor's rate most bonds from the highest ratings — Aaa and AAA respectively — for high grade investment bonds; A and A respectively for medium grade investment bonds; Baa and BBB for lower quality medium grade investment bonds; B and B for speculative issues; Caa and CCC for poor quality issues in danger of default; to C and D respectively which are extremely poor issues in default or close to it. Bonds rated below Baa (Moody's) or BBB (S & P), are classified as junk bonds. The only guarantees of C and D rated bonds are sleepless nights! The two rating systems, though not identical, are similar.

The interest or coupon rates on corporate bonds depends on several factors such as: the quality/risk of the bond (high quality, low risk bonds will have a lower coupon rate than a low quality, high risk bond); the maturity (the longer the bond's maturity, the higher the coupon rate); and the coupon rates of competitors bonds, Treasury bonds, etc.

Not only do the quality and interest rate vary with corporate bonds, there are also different types of issues. There are *secured bonds* which are backed by specific corporate assets in the event of liquidation and *unsecured bonds* which have no pledges of security. To compensate for the high risk of unsecured bonds, the coupon rate on them will be higher than on comparable secured bonds.

Many corporate bonds are callable by the issuing corporation which means the corporation can repurchase bonds at a specified (call) price before maturity. This is of benefit to the corporation (and to the detriment of the investor) because when market rates of interest fall below the coupon rate on the bond, the corporation can call the bonds and reissue them at a lower coupon rate.

Put options allow bondholders to sell their bonds back to the corporation at face value prior to maturity; with *floating rate bonds*, coupon rates adjust with the changes in market rates of interest.

HOW TO BUY

If you buy new issues of bonds, you will pay no commissions since they are absorbed by the issuing corporation or the underwriter of the issue. For existing issues listed on secondary markets, you can buy through

How to Invest   145

brokers who charge commissions ranging from $2.50 to $20 per bond. There are some brokers who will charge a minimum of $30 per bond. These higher commissions are often charged if you buy bonds in odd lots (less than ten bonds).

ADVANTAGES

- You receive a fixed amount of interest on a regular basis. The issuing corporation cannot change the amount and timing of the interest payments regardless of its financial condition — unless it files for bankruptcy.

- You can get capital gains from bonds by purchasing them when interest rates are falling (bond prices and interest rates move in opposite directions). You may also incur capital losses if you have to sell your bonds when interest rates are rising. The volatility of interest rates in the 1980s has provided investors with many trading opportunities for capital gains.

- Your income and principal are relatively safe on high quality corporate bonds.

- You receive a high rate of return relative to other investments; you can increase your current rate of return by purchasing lower quality bonds but they have increased risks of default on interest and principal.

DISADVANTAGES

- Inflation erodes the purchasing power of the fixed interest income payments and the return of principal at maturity.

- Although most high grade listed bonds are marketable, they may not be that liquid because bond prices may be trading at deep discounts to their par (face) values due to rising interest rates and a change in the issuer's ratings.

- You may have difficulty selling your bonds if the issuer's ratings decline and if you have only a small number of bonds to sell.

- A callable bond can be called when you least want your principal returned to you after market interest rates have fallen.

146   Appendix

CAVEATS

Pay attention to the bond's call provisions in order to avoid losses of principal when buying high premium bonds with higher coupon rates than market rates which could be called at lower premium prices.

CONCLUSION

The best time to buy corporate bonds is when interest rates are high so that high yields can be obtained on quality bonds. Bonds should be held when interest rates decline offering potential gains in the upward price movement.

GOVERNMENT AGENCY BONDS

DEFINITION

Government agency securities are issued by federal agencies and government sponsored corporations. Government agency securities are negotiable notes and bonds of the various agencies of the federal government. They are not entirely risk free as they are not the direct obligations of the Treasury, so their yields will be slightly higher than Treasury bonds and notes.

Examples of some agency issues are: Export - Import Bank of the United States; Federal Home Loan Banks; Federal Home Loan Mortgage Corporation, Federal Housing Administration (FHA); Federal National Mortgage Association (FNMA); Government National Mortgage Association (GNMA); Small Business Administration.

FNMA, the Federal Home Loan Mortgage Association and GNMA issue pass through securities. These securities represent an undivided interest in a pool of real estate mortgages. Although there is little risk of default on these securities, there is some uncertainty as to their cash flows. Some of the differences in the pass through securities are highlighted below:

The Government National Mortgage Association (GNMA) is the largest issuer of pass through securities (known as *"Ginnie Maes"*), and is fully guaranteed as to the timely payment of interest and principal by the U.S. government. Ginnie Mae holders receive monthly payments which include both interest and principal since these are pass through mortgage payments which are made by the original borrower of the mortgage. Interest on GNMAs is fully taxable at the federal, state and local government levels.

The Federal Home Loan Corporation also known as *"Freddie Mac,"* is the second largest issuer of mortgage securities called participation certificates. Freddie Mac guarantees the timely payment of interest and recently, with its new program, also guarantees the timely pass through of principal. Freddie Mac securities are not guaranteed by the U.S. government like Ginnie Maes, which is why yields tend to be higher on Freddie Macs than on Ginnie Maes.

The Federal National Mortgage Association (FNMA) known as *"Fannie Mae,"* is a private, stockholder-owned corporation whose shares trade on the New York Stock Exchange. Fannie Mae issues pass through securities which are also not backed by the full credit of the U.S. government and yields tend to be higher than on Ginnie Maes.

Generally, interest on federal agency securities is taxable at all levels (federal, state and local) with some exceptions: Interest received from FHA and Farm Credit agencies is not taxable at the state and local levels.

Other federal agency issues are quoted in the financial newspapers under the Government Agency Bonds section. Maturities of the different agency issues range from twenty-five days to thirty years.

HOW TO BUY

Unlike Treasury securities, new issues of agency securities are not sold by auction but are marketed by the Federal Reserve Bank of New York and its network of dealers. Minimum purchase amounts vary with the different issuing agencies and dealers. For Ginnie Maes, Freddie Macs and Fannie Maes, the minimum purchase of original issues is $25,000, with $5,000 increments thereafter. For some agency securities, the minimum purchase amount may be as low as $1,000. If you buy from a dealer of the syndicate who is underwriting the issue, you will not pay a commission.

If you buy or sell existing federal agency securities on the secondary market, there will be a commission and a spread between the bid and asked prices. These spreads tend to be wider than those of U.S. Treasuries because agency securities are not as actively traded. This greater spread reduces the overall return on investments in agency bonds.

148   Appendix

You can invest indirectly in agency securities through mutual funds or unit pools. This way, investors can invest in smaller amounts; minimum investments can be as low as $1,000. Ginnie Mae mutual funds and investment trusts are good examples.

Ginnie Mae mutual funds differ from Ginnie Mae securities in that the mutual funds are not pass through. With Ginnie Mae securities, you would receive interest and principal payments each month, whereas the mutual fund reinvests the principal and pays dividends from the interest received to its mutual fund shareholders.

Ginnie Mae investment trusts are like closed-end mutual funds where adjustments cannot be made to a portfolio once it is sold — the same as owning Ginnie Mae securities.

Information on agency securities can be obtained from dealer commercial banks, security brokers, the Reserve Bank of New York and issuing agencies.

ADVANTAGES

- Rates of return tend to be higher on government agency securities than on Treasury securities but lower than those offered by corporate bonds.

- Credit risks are good even though agency issues are not guaranteed by the U.S. government. It is unlikely that the U.S. government will allow one of its agencies to default on its obligations.

- If you buy pass-through securities at a discount and mortgagors prepay their mortgage pools, this will increase your rates of return.

- If you buy agency securities when interest rates are high, you will increase your returns if interest rates decline. (The opposite is true if interest rates go up, prices of the securities will decline and returns will be lower than market rates of return.)

- Pass-through securities make payments on a monthly basis giving you the ability to generate greater annual rates than that of a bondholder who receives interest on a semi-annual basis.

- Thirty-year pass-through securities are not as volatile as thirty year Treasuries, due to the fact that part of the principal on pass throughs is repaid monthly.

How to Invest   149

DISADVANTAGES

- Since agency securities are fixed income securities, they are subject to interest rate risk. If you buy a new issue and interest rates go up subsequently, you may not recover the full amount of your investment if you have to sell the security before maturity.

- Agency securities do not protect against rising rates of inflation.

- It is difficult to determine the exact yield for pass through securities due to the uncertainties of the cash flows. Hence, for pass through security holders, monthly checks will vary.

- With pass-through securities, holders receive principal and interest payments. You should not spend your entire monthly checks but rather reinvest a portion of your proceeds to keep your investment capital intact.

CAVEATS

- Avoid buying pass through securities at a premium because if the mortgagors prepay their mortgages, you may lose on the investment or have your return reduced. When interest rates come down, many mortgagors refinance their mortgages at lower rates which means that they will prepay their existing higher rate mortgages.

- If you do buy pass-through securities, avoid small mortgage pools. Invest in large mortgage pools which will reduce the risks of lower returns.

CONCLUSION

Government agency securities provide slightly higher returns than Treasury securities and are considered to be quite safe in terms of credit risk. As with all fixed income securities, buy when interest rates are high to get the best yields.

JUNK BONDS

DEFINITION

Junk bonds (not a misnomer) — also euphemistically referred to as "high yield" bonds — are high risk debt securities. In order to entice investors, the coupon rates of junk bonds are very much higher than the coupon rates of investment grade bonds and Treasury bonds.

Junk bonds have ratings of BBB (Standard & Poor's Corp.), Baa-3 (Moody's Investor Services, Inc.) or lesser categories which means a range of poor quality debt being close to default. Despite their derogatory name, junk bonds have been very popular with investors due to their higher returns. For example, Federated Department Stores' 16-percent coupon bonds due in 1997, offered at par ($1,000) in March of 1987, had dropped to $610 per bond as of April, 1989, which — at that price — would give a buyer a 22-percent yield (assuming that Federated continued to pay all interest and repay the principal) (Winkler, 1989b).

Issuers of junk bonds offer these higher coupon yields for two major reasons: they may be financially troubled and junk bonds may be one of the few avenues left to raise funds, and corporations may use junk bonds to finance takeovers of other corporations. The latter reason has accounted for the recent growth in the junk bond market. Bear in mind, however, that the risks of default on these issues are much greater for both the leveraged buyouts and financially troubled corporations, despite many studies done by brokerage firms touting the relative safety of high yield junk bonds.

In an unpublished study by Harvard Professor Paul Asquith and two colleagues, the authors claim that the risks of default on junk bonds are significantly higher than those quoted by published studies. (Winkler, 1989a). According to Winkler (1989a), the significant difference between the Harvard study and the other published studies on junk bonds is that the Harvard study measures defaults over the life of the bonds. This increases the default rate because it is low in the early years of a bond and rises over the life of the bond. In previously published studies, the default rate was obtained by dividing the number of defaults by the total number of outstanding junk bonds. The low number of defaults obtained this way is due to several factors — mainly the explosive growth in the number of junk bonds issued.

Although investors in junk bonds have received higher returns than those of other fixed income securities, they face risks other than the overhanging specter of default:

How to Invest   151

- there is the risk that as market rates of interest drop, the issuers of junk bonds will either buy them back or call them and refinance them with lower yield debt;

- with the increasing nervousness over junk bond defaults, the market prices of junk bonds have tumbled, meaning that if you wanted to sell your bonds you would lose part of your initial investment (the selling price of the bonds would be lower than the acquisition price);

- junk bond investors may have difficulty selling their bonds on the market in that there may be no buyers for them (Winkler, 1989c).

You should carefully weigh the trade-off between these and other risks versus the "promised" higher returns, keeping in mind that there are no (or very few) "free lunches" on Wall Street.

HOW TO BUY

If you buy newly issued junk bonds, you will pay no commissions since these are absorbed by the issuing corporation or the underwriter of the issue. However, before investing, you should study the company's prospectus (which should always be made available to potential investors when a publicly listed company sells securities) to assess the overall risks. From the financial statements, you can determine:

- the level of debt (the percentage of debt to total assets);

- the number of debt issues senior to this issue (in the case of bankruptcy, the greater the number of senior debt issues, the lower the priority of the junk bond investor's claims);

- whether the level of earnings will cover the interest payments on all the debt issues including the one to be financed.

If the company does not have sufficient earnings from operations to service its debt and may need to sell off assets to generate funds, you should be very wary of investing. Similarly, warning flags should go up if the debt to total assets ratio is excessively high and the proceeds of this issue will be used to pay off maturing issues.

You can buy existing issues of junk bonds which are listed on the bond exchanges through brokers who charge commissions ranging from

152   Appendix

$2.50 to $20 per bond. There are some brokers who will charge a minimum of $30 per bond. These higher commissions are often charged if investors buy bonds in odd lots (less than ten bonds). For existing issues, you will not see a prospectus, but before investing you should request the latest company information from your broker.

Instead of investing in individual bonds, you can invest in mutual funds with high-yield portfolios. The advantages of mutual funds are diversification (for a small investment you will have a share in a diversified portfolio as opposed to buying bonds of different companies at a significant cost to achieve adequate diversification), professional management and research. As to the latter, there are no guarantees that professional fund managers will do any better than individuals in choosing bond issues. Moreover, with the recent turmoil in the junk bond markets, billions of investor dollars have been exiting the junk bond mutual funds further weakening the prices of the junk bond mutual funds (Siconolfi, 1989).

ADVANTAGES

- You receive a higher yield than from other fixed income securities — the rewards for taking risks.

- When market interest rates are going down, you have opportunities for capital gains (when the selling price of the bond exceeds the purchase price of the bond).

- Nervousness about defaults in the junk bond market has driven the prices of junk bonds down as if they are all going to default, which presents opportunities for capital gains and high yields for those investors willing to take risks in buying the better quality issues at low prices.

DISADVANTAGES

- You face higher risks of default on interest and principal with junk bonds than with better quality debt.

- You may experience illiquidity in trying to sell your junk bonds if the ratings of the issuer decline further due to nervousness in the bond market or specifically due to bad news concerning the issuer.

How to Invest   153

- When interest rates fall, companies that can afford to will buy back their high-yield bonds and replace them with lower yielding debt.

- You may see an erosion of your capital when the prices of high-yield bonds slide due to nervousness concerning the junk bond market.

CAVEATS:

- Avoid high yield bonds that are part of small issues (less than $75 million) and are not listed on an exchange (Peers, 1988).

- Avoid buying bonds with the highest yields, bearing in mind that the higher the yield, the greater the risk.

CONCLUSION

Investing in junk bonds is not for "unsophisticated" investors but for those who are able to analyze the financial statements of companies in order to differentiate the "quality" high yield issues from those that are descending along the path to bankruptcy.

MUNICIPAL BONDS

DEFINITION

Municipal bonds are those issued by state and local governments and certain public authorities. Municipal bonds differ from all other bonds in that they are exempt from federal income taxes and when issued in your state are exempt from state and local taxes.

The most common type of municipal bond is the *general obligation bond* which is also the safest of the municipals. Issuers of general obligation bonds are states and local governments. Revenues from these issues are used to finance schools, roads and capital expenditures. Interest payments and the repayment of the debt are relatively assured since the issuer can create revenues through their taxing power.

The other major type of municipal bond is the *revenue bond*. These are issued to finance specific projects and are repaid from the income earned on the projects. Revenue bondholders do not have any claims to

154   Appendix

the tax receipts of the issuer, so in recessionary times, you should stick to buying those revenue bonds which finance essential services. In other words, for maximum safety, you should avoid those revenue bonds issued for non-essential services such as hotels, sports complexes, etc.

Municipal bonds are rated by commercial rating companies (Standard & Poor's, Moody's, etc.) just as corporate bonds are. Although municipal bonds are considered to be relatively safe, there have been a number of defaults and there are currently many cities that have had their bonds downgraded. (At the time of this writing, for example, the city of Philadelphia has had their bonds downgraded.) The risks of municipal bonds vary considerably, but general obligation bonds are generally less risky than revenue bonds, despite Philadelphia's bond woes.

Currently, the yield spread between lower and higher quality municipals is relatively small. According to Slater and Herman (1990) the yield spread between AAA rated municipals and Baa municipals is less than 1/2 a percentage point. In recessionary times, it makes sense to go for higher quality municipals because even if the state or local governments do not default on their issues, their ratings may go down, resulting in a lower market price for the debt. Yields on municipal bonds are lower than corporate bonds due to their tax exempt status.

The most important feature of municipal bonds is tax exemption. Most municipal bonds are exempt from federal taxes and state (and local) taxes if issued in that state (and locality). With the passing of the Tax Reform Act of 1986, certain private activity bonds which have been issued for nonessential purposes (sports complexes, industrial parks, parking complexes, etc.) are no longer exempt from federal income taxes. Similarly, interest on *industrial development bonds* (IDBs) issued after August 7, 1986, is treated as a preference item which may trigger the alternate minimum tax for individuals. The alternate minimum tax is 24 percent for 1991. Industrial development bonds are issues where 10 percent of the proceeds are used by private companies.

If municipal bonds can reduce income taxes, they should be evaluated against the returns of regular bonds. In other words, compare the yields of municipals with the yields of corporate bonds of similar quality to see which is more advantageous.

The before tax return of a municipal bond can be calculated as follows:

$$\text{Before Tax Return} \quad = \quad \frac{\text{Tax Free Yield}}{(1 - \text{Tax Rate})}$$

How to Invest   155

A 6-percent coupon municipal bond bought by an investor in the 28-percent marginal tax bracket will have a before tax return of 8.33 percent:

$$\text{Before Tax Return} = \frac{6 \text{ percent}}{(1 - .28)}$$

$$= 8.33 \text{ percent}$$

This municipal bond with a before tax return of 8.33 percent can be compared to other fixed income securities of similar quality whose yields would have to be greater than this to be a better investment. Bear in mind that if this bond is also exempt from state and local taxes, the before tax return will be greater than 8.33 percent.

Zero-coupon municipal bonds have become popular since the Tax Reform Act of 1986. They are sold at a deep discount and redeemed at face value ($1,000) at maturity. Interest received at maturity is exempt from federal taxes. Stripped zero-coupon municipal bonds are sold by large brokerage firms. See the section on Zero-Coupon Bonds for an explanation of stripped bonds.

HOW TO BUY

Municipal bonds can be bought through brokers in units of $5,000 or $10,000, although many brokers require minimum purchases of $25,000 to $100,000. Those who do buy small numbers of bonds (odd lots) will end up paying a greater *commission* and/or *spread*. A spread is the difference between the bid and ask price of the bond, while a commission is the charge for buying or selling the bond.

There is an active secondary market for existing municipal bonds which is supported by municipal bond dealers. Some of the active existing revenue bonds are quoted in the *Wall Street Journal*. If you are interested in existing general obligation bonds, you should call your brokers to see what they have available.

You may also buy new issues through dealer-syndicates. The advantages of buying new issues are that no sales commissions are charged. New municipal issues are advertised in the *Wall Street Journal* and other national publications.

Commissions — or spreads — vary as to the number of bonds purchased or the amount invested. Rather than purchase individual bonds, small investors may prefer to invest in municipal bond *mutual funds* or municipal bond *unit trusts*, both of which offer greater diversification.

156   Appendix

A unit trust is a closed-end fund with a fixed portfolio of bonds which are held until maturity (or until called). The yield or return is fixed.

In a mutual fund, bonds may be bought and sold by the investment company. You can reinvest by buying more shares or you can liquidate all or part of your investments by selling shares at their market prices. Share prices react to changing interest rates and the yields of the fund will also change over time. Mutual funds would be the better choice for someone with a shorter investment period, whereas unit trusts are geared to a long-term buy and hold strategy particularly if the trust is bought when the initial yield is high.

ADVANTAGES

- The interest on most municipals is exempt from federal income tax. In addition, interest may be exempt from state and local taxes when issued in that state and locality. This increases the before tax yield.

- For income dependent investors, it provides regular interest income.

DISADVANTAGES

- Municipal bonds do not protect against inflation due to their fixed income.

- Bond prices fluctuate with changes in market rates of interest. The market prices of longer maturity bonds fluctuate more than shorter maturity bonds.

- Good quality municipal bonds are relatively safe; the risk of default is of increasing concern, however, due to a number of defaults in the past and the increasing number of financially troubled cities.

- Many high coupon municipals have a call provision. If buying municipals on the secondary market, be careful if you pay a premium on a high coupon bond. First check to see if it has a call provision.

- Municipal bonds are less liquid than government securities. It may be difficult to sell some of the smaller, less active municipal bonds in the secondary market.

CAVEATS

- Municipal bonds are not entirely risk free. Buy municipals with the highest quality ratings and stay away from small unrated issues and speculative revenue bonds.

- When buying a new issue, check the legal opinion which is attached to the offering circular.

CONCLUSION

If, after considering taxes, municipal bonds are advantageous, buy high quality obligation bonds. Unfortunately, tax advantages can easily be swept away with the stroke of a congressional pen.

TREASURY BONDS AND NOTES

DEFINITION

Treasury notes (T-notes) and *Treasury bonds* (T-bonds) are issued by the federal government as a means of borrowing funds. Treasury notes have maturities ranging from two to ten years, whereas Treasury bonds have maturities ranging from ten to thirty years. Both T-notes and T-bonds are available in *registered, bearer* or *book entry* form. With book entry form, an investor would receive a statement showing the amount of T-bonds or T-notes owned rather than actual T-bond or T-note certificates.

Treasury notes are not callable, whereas outstanding Treasury bonds may be (usually called in the last five years before maturity). They both may be issued in denominations as low as $1,000 to encourage sales from individual investors. However, for certain issues of T-notes, $1,000 denominations have not been available; the minimum has been $5,000.

Interest on both T-notes and T-bonds is paid semi-annually. Since these are direct obligations of the federal government, there is virtually no risk of default. Investors who would like to earn higher yields than those offered by the Treasuries should check the yields of bonds offered by U.S. government agencies (GNMAs, FNMAs). These could yield as much as 1 percent more than Treasury obligations.

Some Treasury bonds, such as the 3-percent coupon bonds maturing on February 15, 1995, and the 3 1/2-percent coupon bonds maturing on November 15, 1998, are very different from the rest of the Treasuries. These issues, called *"flower bonds,"* are used to settle federal estate

158   Appendix

taxes because of their favorable tax treatment status. If an individual decedent owned $200,000 of par value of these flower bonds and the decedent's estate owed $200,000 in federal estate taxes, these bonds would be accepted by the Internal Revenue Service at par value, even though they may be worth less on the market. Generally, these bonds sell at a discount due to their low coupon rates.

The Treasury department does impose some conditions when flower bonds are used to settle federal tax liabilities. If there is a gain at the time of the decedent's death, it will be taxed as a capital gain. Flower bonds are no longer issued by the Treasury. Your situation should be discussed with a tax advisor if you are considering using flower bonds for tax planning purposes.

Many of the brokerage firms, in the 1980s, packaged U. S Treasuries in the form of zero-coupon Treasury packages, such as *CATS* and *TIGRS* This was followed by the Treasury's own *STRIPS* packages. (See Zero-Coupon bonds for a more detailed description.)

HOW TO BUY

There is an active secondary market composed of dealers. Due to the wide range of maturities, you may find many outstanding issues trading at a discount. You can either buy new issues of Treasury bonds and notes or existing issues through your brokers or bankers. Ask   your brokers/bankers for a dealer's quote sheet to see what existing issues are available.

You can also buy new issues directly from the government, thereby avoiding the transaction fees charged when buying through a broker or banker. Watch the financial newspapers for announcements of upcoming auctions or call the Federal Reserve Bank to find out the dates of upcoming issues. Ask to be put on a mailing list to receive notification of issues. New issues of two year T-notes are auctioned monthly but longer term T-notes and T-bonds are generally auctioned the second month of every quarter.

When you want to buy directly from the Federal Reserve Bank, you will need to fill out a tender form to submit to the Federal Reserve Bank or its branches. You will also need to submit a check (or any other approved form of payment) with the form.

Bids can be either in the form of a competitive or a non-competitive bid. More sophisticated investors submit competitive bids which are bid yields to two decimal places. For instance, if you anticipate the bid yield to be 8.25 percent, the bid would be accepted if it is close to the stop out bid determined by the Treasury. Thus, competitive bidders run the risk of having their bids rejected or even accepted at lower returns than other investors. This means that they will be paying a higher price for the issue.

To avoid these risks, you can submit non-competitive bids indicating that you will accept the average yield that results for the auction.

Treasury obligations, which are held to maturity, can be redeemed at no cost at a Federal Reserve Bank. Or, you can choose to roll over the maturing T-bonds or T-notes into a bid for a new issue. Banks or brokers will also redeem issues at maturity for a fee.

If you do not want to wait until the issues mature, there is an active secondary market. The dealer spreads (difference between the bid and asked prices) are the lowest among the fixed-income securities and can be sold through bankers or brokers.

ADVANTAGES

- Interest received on T-notes and T-bonds is exempt from state and local taxes.

- There is virtually no risk of default since they are obligations of the federal government.

- T-notes and T-bonds are extremely liquid due to the active secondary market.

- Some issues of T-notes and T-bonds have lower purchase minimums than T-bills ($10,000) making them affordable for small investors.

DISADVANTAGES

- For the longer maturity T-bonds (ten to thirty years), there is interest rate risk. If interest rates go up after long-term bonds are bought, the market price of the bonds will be depressed. You could lose a significant amount of money if forced to sell before maturity.

- The longer maturity issues do not protect against rising rates of inflation.

- Interest rates have been quite volatile and investors could buy thirty year, 8 1/4-percent T-bonds at present, only to find that in the near future, coupons of equivalent maturity T-bonds could go up to 13 percent.

160   Appendix

CAVEATS

Avoid longer maturities unless you feel confident that both interest rates and inflation will go down in the future.

CONCLUSION

Treasury bonds and notes are safe investments for those who can afford to buy and hold them to maturity. Since there are so many maturities to choose from, ownership can be staggered to provide steady income over a period of time.

ZERO-COUPON BONDS

DEFINITION

Zero-coupon bonds are debt securities that pay no periodic interest but are issued at a deep discount and redeemed at face value ($1,000) at maturity. For example, a $1,000 twenty-year zero-coupon bond yielding 10 percent would cost about $148 at issuance. You receive no interest but, having bought the bond at a large discount, receive a return through the appreciation of the bond's price as it gets closer to maturity. This appreciation is not treated as a capital gain but as compound interest. The Internal Revenue Service taxes the bondholder on annual interest that accrues each year as if it were paid out. Thus, you pay federal taxes on the earned interest even though you will only receive the money when the bonds mature or when they are sold. This is the primary reason why zero-coupon bonds may have little or no interest to many investors. However, zero-coupon bonds are much more attractive as part of IRAs, Keogh Plans and pension plans where accrued interest is only taxed when funds are withdrawn.

The quality of the issuer of zero-coupon bonds is important since the return to you depends on:

- the issuer's ability to redeem the bonds at maturity, or

- to sell them before maturity at a higher price than the purchase price (since the amount originally invested is assumed to grow due to the time value of money).

The safest zero-coupon bonds are those offered directly by the U.S. Treasury and they have the added advantage of being non-callable. U.S. Treasury securities can also be packaged by brokerage firms and mar-

How to Invest   161

keted as zero-coupon bonds known by acronyms such as *TIGRS*, *CATS* and *LIONS*. These are referred to as *STRIPS*. Brokerage firms will buy Treasury bonds and then sell zero-coupon bond certificates of varying maturities to investors. U.S. Treasury bonds are held in escrow. When the brokerage firms receive the interest, they do not pass it on to the zero-coupon holders but use the interest to pay off any maturing zero coupon bonds. Although not entirely free of risk, STRIPS offer a high degree of security due to the escrowing of the Treasury bonds. Strips also have the advantage of being non-callable. They are less liquid than Treasury zeros but generally offer a slightly higher yield.

Corporate zero-coupon bonds tend to be riskier. Mostly the yield does not compensate for the higher risks and should be avoided.

Zero-coupon municipal bonds are those issued by state and local governments and the accrued interest is not taxed at the federal level (only when the zero-coupon bond is sold is the gain taxed at the federal level). Thus, municipal zero-coupon bonds alleviate the tax problems of zero-coupon bonds issued by the Treasury and corporations. The disadvantage of zero municipals is that some are callable, meaning investors can be paid off when they least want to be.

Zero-coupon bonds — like other fixed income securities — are sensitive to market rates of interest and tend to be more volatile than conventional bonds. According to James M. Benham of Capital Management Group, when interest rates fall, zero-coupon bonds will appreciate more than existing conventional bonds (Rowland, 1989). However, when interest rates rise, the price of zero-coupons can fall significantly. The longer the maturity of zero-coupon bonds, the greater the risk of loss due to changes in interest rates.

HOW TO BUY

Zero-coupon securities may be bought through securities brokers, dealers and banks. New issues of zero-coupon bonds may be bought through brokers who underwrite the issue and involve no direct costs to the buyers. However, when buying existing zero-coupon bonds in the secondary market, brokers will charge a spread (asking slightly higher than market price), and when selling, offer a slightly lower than market price. Spreads on zero-coupon bonds can vary significantly among brokers; before buying, it is important to shop around to minimize the spread. Generally, the minimum number of zero-coupon bonds that a dealer/broker will handle in any transaction is ten.

You may choose to put your money in mutual funds that specialize in zero-coupon bonds. Advantages of mutual funds include: professional management, simplified record keeping for tax purposes, funds with

162   Appendix

different maturities, low per share costs and the ease of being able to move in and out of the funds. As with all mutual funds, however, fees which can be quite high are deducted from the net assets. Thus, investors who intend to invest in zero coupons and hold them to maturity would improve their returns by buying individual zero-coupon bonds rather than mutual funds.

ADVANTAGES

- Zero-coupon bonds appreciate faster than conventional bonds when market interest rates decline. (See the disadvantages when market interest rates go up).

- Zero-coupon securities are excellent vehicles for IRAs, Keogh accounts and pension plans due to their tax-deferred growth and predictable amounts at maturity.

DISADVANTAGES

- There is a tax consequence of having to pay taxes annually on accrued interest which is not received until maturity.

- Zero-coupon bond prices are extremely volatile: when interest rates go up, zero-coupon bond prices may plunge significantly, resulting in large capital losses. (See the advantages when market interest rates go down).

- When interest rates do go up, you are not able to benefit because you have no coupon income to reinvest.

- If a zero-coupon bond defaults, there is more to lose than on a conventional bond because with the latter you would have received some interest which could have been reinvested.

CAVEATS

- Since transaction costs (spreads that brokers charge) can be high when buying and selling zero-coupon bonds, calculate the yield after transaction costs and compare it to the after transaction yield of Treasury bonds of similar maturities. If the difference is not significant, you may be better off with Treasury bonds (Donnelly, 1989).

How to Invest   163

- Be prepared to hold the bonds to maturity, if you do not successfully guess the direction of interest rates.

- Spread your interest rate risks by buying zero-coupon bonds with different maturities because the longer the maturity the greater the price volatility.

CONCLUSION

Zero-coupon bonds are suitable long-term investment vehicles for retirement accounts (to avoid paying taxes on interest not received) and for financing specific goals such as college tuition. Currently, tax advantages are available when zero-coupon bonds are bought in the names of children; these advantages should be discussed with a tax advisor.

3   CLOSED-END FUNDS

DEFINITION

Investment companies offer two types of funds, *closed-end* and *open-end*. Closed-end funds sell a fixed number of shares and use the proceeds to invest in stocks and/or bonds, whereas with open-end funds (also known as mutual funds) investment companies continuously offer new shares to investors and redeem shares from investors. With closed-end funds, investment companies do not redeem shares from investors who want to sell, thus the number of shares remains constant.

Most of the closed-end funds trade on the New York Stock Exchange (e.g., Korea Fund, Japan Fund, ASA Ltd) and the American Stock Exchange, while some trade on over-the-counter markets, where shareholders may buy and sell their shares. The publicly traded closed-end funds are regulated by the Securities and Exchange Commission (SEC).

Some closed-end funds specialize in stocks or bonds or in industry sectors (e.g., ASA Ltd in gold mining stocks, Emerging Medical Technology Fund, Petroleum and Resources Corporation), convertible securities or municipal bonds, while others invest in a combination of securities.

The prices of closed-end funds shares are determined by supply and demand on the market. These funds generally trade either at a discount (below the net asset value of the portfolio) or at a premium

164   Appendix

(above the net asset value). The net asset value of a fund is the total market value of the assets (minus any liabilities) divided by the fixed number of shares outstanding. Mostly, the prices of these funds will be close to their net asset values, although it is not uncommon to find discounts and premiums ranging to 30 percent of net asset values.

The dual purpose fund is a special type of closed-end fund that issues two classes of stock: one type to common stockholders who receive all the capital gains realized on the sale of securities in the fund and another to preferred stockholders who receive all the interest and dividends produced by the securities in the fund.

HOW TO INVEST

You may buy and sell shares of closed-end funds through security brokers (some security brokers specialize in these funds). Information on these funds can be found in Value Line Investment Survey, Standard and Poor's Record Sheets, Moody's Finance Manuals, Weisenberger's Investment Companies (in most public libraries), and other similar investment sources.

You can find the share prices of the listed closed-end funds in the stock exchange sections of the daily newspapers. *Barron's*, a weekly financial newspaper lists the net asset values, the share prices and the discounts or premiums of the stock and bond closed-end funds, as well as the dual purpose funds.

Request information from your brokers or research the particular fund before you buy into it.

ADVANTAGES

- You have opportunities to buy into closed-end funds trading at discounts (below net asset value) which offer the potential of capital gains (and on the downside — capital losses). Some investment advisors and brokers suggest buying closed-end funds with large discounts by historical standards and selling them when they have small discounts or premiums.

- The larger actively traded closed-end funds give you the benefits of liquidity in that you can easily buy and sell your shares on the stock exchanges. (The less actively traded funds will be less liquid).

How to Invest   165

DISADVANTAGES

- There is the risk that the value of the fund shares can move independently of the value of the securities being held in the fund's portfolio. For example, you may sell your shares in the closed-end fund thus driving the price down despite the fact that the assets in the fund are doing well. This represents a buy opportunity when the fund's shares trade at a discount to its net asset values.

- The brokerage commissions together with management fees and expenses can be high, thereby reducing the returns closed-end funds can produce.

- If you want to buy or sell a small number of shares (less than 100 shares is an odd lot) the commissions charged to execute the transaction will be high.

CAVEATS

- You should become familiar with all the fees charged by the investment company before buying into the fund.

- Avoid buying into funds when they are first offered to the public because a portion of your initial funds will go toward paying underwriting fees and selling commissions. For example, if you pay $10 a share and seventy cents goes towards these expenses, the net asset value will fall to $9.30 directly after issuance.

- Compare the long-term performance of closed-end funds before investing — some have really not done terribly well and you may want to avoid those with poor long-term records.

CONCLUSION

Many investment advisors suggest buying into closed-end funds when their shares are trading at deep discounts to their net asset values and selling when the discounts narrow or rise to a premium.

You should also look out for closed-end funds that are to be converted to open-end funds, which means that if their shares are trading at a discount, they will rise to their net asset values at the date of conversion.

166   Appendix

If you want to avoid the market risks of closed-end funds, consider open-end (mutual) funds.

4   COMMON STOCK

DEFINITION

Common stock represents ownership in a corporation. For example, if a company has 1,000 shares of common stock outstanding and you buy 100 shares, you are entitled to a 10-percent share of control (usually through voting rights) and profits; and in the case of liquidation, a 10 percent share of the net proceeds (after creditors and preferred shareholders have been paid).

The profits of the company are either retained or paid out as dividends to shareholders. Companies whose shares are listed on the exchanges (New York Stock Exchange, American Stock Exchange, over-the-counter markets and/or regional exchanges) have market values based on factors such as, investors' expectations of future company earnings, dividends, growth in the industry, business and market climate and economic conditions. Prices of shares can fluctuate considerably due to conditions other than the financial status of the company.

Blue-chip stocks (stocks of well established, financially secure companies) are mostly listed on the New York Stock Exchange. These stocks tend to have histories of regular earnings and dividends and their market prices are less volatile than growth stocks. *Growth stocks* are stocks of new, young companies which are listed on the over-the-counter markets, the NASDAQ National Market and on the American Exchange. Many of these growth stocks are in high technology industries where risks are greater, resulting in greater fluctuations in stock prices.

HOW TO BUY

You can buy and sell common stock through securities brokers and of late through many banks and financial institutions. Although the latter may not offer the same full range of services as a brokerage firm, commissions may be lower. Commissions depend on both the amount invested and the number of shares in the transaction. Commissions vary considerably among brokerage firms, discount brokers, banks, etc., and you should compare these charges along with the services provided to see whether the higher commissions are warranted.

Some of the services provided by brokerage firms include: investment advice, information and research reports. Brokers will send copies of information about specific companies (which they purchase from Value Line Investment Survey, Moody's, Standard & Poor's, etc.) to interested investors.

You can also obtain information about specific companies by calling or writing the company directly and asking for their annual report which includes the financial statements, auditors report, chairmans report, the general outlook and future prospects (as reported by the company). More detailed than the annual report is the 10-K report (filed with the SEC) which also may be requested from the company.

Most public libraries subscribe to rating services such as Moody's, Standard & Poor's, Value Line Investment Survey, as well as the major business newspapers (*Wall Street Journal, Barron's, Investor's Business Daily*) and magazines (*Business Week, Forbes, Fortune*).

ADVANTAGES

- Over the long term, common stocks have provided higher returns than long-term U.S. bonds and Treasury bills (Slater, 1989), although over the short term, the prices of stocks can be more volatile.

- Common stocks provide a better hedge against a moderate level of inflation over the long run than bonds due to the fact that share prices generally rise in value and dividends are increased due to inflation.

- Actively traded common stocks of publicly held companies can be sold quickly and converted easily to cash.

- Common stock affords you the opportunity for capital gains (or capital losses) through appreciation (depreciation) of the price of the stock from purchase to sale. Although capital gains are currently taxed as ordinary income, the capital gains/losses provisions have been left in the Internal Revenue Tax Code. Should income tax rates rise in the future, this could cause the reinstatement of lower capital gains rates which would be advantageous for investors in higher marginal tax brackets.

DISADVANTAGES

- There is the risk that you could lose part of your investment through the decline in the market price of common stocks (some stocks are more volatile than others and therefore risk-

168   Appendix

ier). For example, you may need the money and be forced to sell your common stocks when the market is depressed.

- The market price of common stocks can fluctuate widely on a daily basis due to factors such as large buy/sell orders, rumors and unrelated business conditions such as economic (interest rates in the economy, inflation, budget deficits, trade deficits, etc.) and political factors.

- Dividends are not guaranteed. Dividends are declared at the discretion of the company's board of directors; if earnings go down and/or alternative uses are found internally for those funds, dividends will not be declared.

- If a company goes bankrupt, common shareholders could lose their entire investment since they are the last to be paid (first are the creditors, followed by preferred stockholders and then common stockholders).

CAVEATS

For every story of sudden wealth from buying stocks, there are many more of loss situations. Take care in the selection of stocks. Research the stocks according to their earnings and growth potential, their security and quality, before buying. Conservative investors may want to avoid stocks which have low ratings (B or less by Moody's or Standard & Poor's).

Select a broker or brokerage firm that has a good reputation and one that meets your needs. Bear in mind that a broker makes a living from commissions due to buying and selling, so be wary of the broker whose strategy is frequent buying and selling.

Compare commission charges of the different brokers — they vary significantly.

CONCLUSION

Common stocks are not for investors who cannot tolerate the risks of stock price fluctuations and volatility of returns. For those willing to buy common stocks in anticipation of capital appreciation who do not want to manage them, mutual funds which invest in common stocks may be the answer. Mutual funds decrease the financial risks through diversification by investing in a broad spectrum of stocks. Individual investors,

How to Invest   169

however, may not have sufficient resources to buy enough stocks to diversify their risks.

A good time to buy common stocks is when the economy is prospering and interest rates are low — when businesses generally experience greater growth and profits.

Common stocks are good investments if you have funds to invest for a long time, where stocks can be left to appreciate and ride out any short-term fluctuations in the market.

5   CONVERTIBLE SECURITIES

DEFINITION

Convertible securities are bonds or preferred stock which can be exchanged for common stock of the issuing company at the option of the holder.

The convertible bondholder (or convertible preferred stockholder) has the right to convert each bond or preferred stock within a specified time period into a fixed number of shares of common stock, regardless of that stock's market price. For example, if a convertible bond of XYZ Corporation, which sells at $1,000, can be converted into twenty shares of common stock (a conversion ratio of twenty) then the conversion price for each share of common stock is $50 (1000/20). The conversion price is set above the current price of the common stock when the convertible is issued (it's not unusual to find a 20-percent premium). Should the market price of XYZ Corporation's common stock rise to $70 a share, the holder could convert the bond into $1,400 worth of common stock (20 × $70). The market price will also rise to $1,400. Thus, the convertible bond will be trading at a premium which is most often the case for convertibles. The premium on convertibles is what an investor is willing to pay in return for the higher yields (from the interest on bonds and dividends on preferred stock) than what is earned on common stock, as well as the ability to participate in the capital appreciation of the common stock. Generally, the same holds true for convertible preferred stock and convertible bonds except that the conversion ratio of preferred stock is small. For example, one share of preferred for one share of common, or two shares of preferred for one share of common.

The market value of a convertible bond/preferred stock depends on the market price of the common stock for the upside potential appreciation. For the downside value, it would not decline more than what it would be worth as a straight bond or preferred share. As discussed in

170   Appendix

the earlier example of XYZ Corporation, when the market price of the common stock rises substantially above the conversion price, the price of the convertible bond/preferred stock will be equal to the price of the common stock. On the downside, when the market price of the common stock is below the conversion price, the convertible will be priced no lower than a straight bond or preferred stock of comparable risk and yield.

Market prices of bonds and convertible securities are sensitive to interest rates. If interest rates in the economy rise above the coupon rate of the bond, the price of the bond and convertible securities will fall. The coupon rate is the interest payment per annum as a percentage of the bonds par value (generally $1,000). The converse is true if market interest rates fall below the coupon rate of the bond/convertible security, the price of the bond/convertible will rise.

HOW TO BUY

Convertible securities may be purchased through full-service brokerage firms, discount brokers and brokerage services offered by banks. Investors may purchase new issues of convertible securities from the investment banker that underwrites the issue or through participating brokers.

Most of the convertible bonds are listed on the over-the-counter markets while the convertible bonds of the larger, better known companies are listed on the New York Bond Exchange. (The same applies to convertible preferred stocks — listings on over-the-counter markets, American Stock Exchange and New York Stock Exchange).

Brokerage fees charged for purchasing convertible bonds would be very similar to those charged for buying regular bonds. Commissions charged per bond could range from $2.50 to $20 depending on the number of bonds purchased, the total value of the purchase and the type of broker (full service or discount). Some brokers charge a minimum of $30 per bond and may have a minimum number of bonds per transaction (this varies from ten to 100 bonds).

Fees for convertible preferred stock would be similar to buying common stock. Fees and spreads would be higher for purchasing in odd lots (for preferred convertible stock an odd lot would be less than 100 shares for the higher priced convertible preferred stocks).

You may invest indirectly in convertibles by buying shares of mutual funds that specialize in convertible securities. This saves you from analyzing the various convertible securities to find the most attractive issues. The advantages of mutual funds are that they have professional management and you will have a share in a diversified portfolio

of convertibles. Most individual investors may not have sufficient resources to buy many different convertible issues to diversify their risks.

A wealth of information about convertible securities can be found
in: the weekly *Value Line Convertibles Report* put out by Value Line
Investment Survey; the section on convertible bonds in the *Standard &
Poor's Bond Guide;* convertible preferred stocks in the *Standard &
Poor's Stock Guide*; as well as research information from brokerage
companies.

ADVANTAGES

- Convertible securities offer the upside potential of capital gains
  through the appreciation of common stock and the reduced
  downside risk if the market price of the common stock falls
  below the conversion value, in that the convertible will be
  valued no less than as a straight bond/preferred stock.

- Interest (dividends) received on convertible bonds (preferred
  stock) generally exceeds the dividends paid by comparable
  common stock. Some corporations that have convertible securities may not pay dividends on their common stock and corporations that do could easily eliminate them if they have a
  drop in earnings. Failure to pay interest on debt, however,
  would force the company into bankruptcy.

- Convertible securities offer some protection against inflation
  since the market prices of both common stock and convertible
  bonds rise with inflation. However, if conversion does not take
  place — when the market price of the common stock does not
  rise above the conversion value — you have no protection from
  inflation as interest/dividends received on convertible securities are fixed.

DISADVANTAGES

- Yields on convertible securities are often lower than yields on
  regular bonds.

- In the event of liquidation, convertible bonds frequently are
  subordinated to other debt in their claim on the issuing
  corporation's assets. Convertible preferred shareholders would
  be paid after creditors but before common shareholders. Risk

172   Appendix

would depend on the overall strength of the issuing corporation.

- Convertible securities being fixed income securities are sensitive to changes in market rates of interest. The price of convertible securities will fluctuate as interest rates change.

- When interest rates in the economy fall, there is an increased risk that the convertible bonds will be called by the issuing company. The issuing company can then refinance their convertibles with cheaper debt.

- You may face the risks of dilution of the common stock of the company. This occurs when the value of the common stock decreases due to an increase in the number of common shares outstanding through conversion or new issues of common stock.

- In the case of a leveraged buy out of the company, you may end up with a nonconvertible security which has a lower yield than the company's other bonds.

CAVEATS

- Do not buy a company's convertible securities unless you would be willing to buy that company's common stock. If the convertible security is never converted to common stock, the interest/dividends received on the convertible will be less than if you had invested in a straight bond.

- Be wary of buying convertibles which are trading at high premiums over both the market values of the common stock and/or the callable price of the convertibles.

- Check the provisions of the convertibles before you buy, such as, whether or not there is a sinking fund that will allow the issuing company to redeem a specific number of convertibles each year, the call price, etc.

CONCLUSION

Convertible securities offer potential appreciation and fixed income but they may not be the best of both worlds. Convertibles allow you to hedge your bets in both the debt and equities markets. Generally, convertible securities will do best when interest rates are falling and the stock market is rising.

6   MUTUAL FUNDS (OPEN-END FUNDS)

DEFINITION

Mutual funds are operated by investment companies that make investments on behalf of their shareholders. Individuals and institutional investors invest their money in these funds by buying shares at their *net asset values* (NAV). The net asset value price of the share equals the total assets minus the liabilities of the fund divided by the number of outstanding shares. The money received is invested in specific assets (common stocks, bonds, Treasury bonds, international stocks, etc.) which would depend on the fund's objectives.

Mutual funds can be *open-end* or *closed-end*. With open-end funds, the number of shares can increase or decrease with purchases of new shares and sales of existing shares, whereas with closed-end funds, the number of shares is limited to the number in the initial issue. (See the section on closed-end funds for more information). Shares in open-end funds can be bought and sold at their net asset values.

There are many types of mutual funds, each with its own objectives. See Table A.1 for a listing of some of the types of mutual funds. Although there are many different types of open-end mutual funds, they do share some common characteristics:

- The net asset value price of each fund is calculated at the end of each business day and reported in the financial section of the daily newspapers, under "Mutual Funds."

- You can sell your shares back to the investment company at the net asset value and can purchase additional shares from the investment company at the net asset value.

- When investing in a "family of funds" such as Vanguard, Fidelity, etc., you can switch your money from a common stock fund, for example, to a bond fund or any other fund in that investment company's group of funds.

Mutual funds can be grouped into four broad categories: *money market funds, stock funds, bond funds* and other funds such as commodity funds.

174   Appendix

Table A.1   Types of Funds

FUND	OBJECTIVE
Aggressive Growth Funds	Seek maximum capital gains. Invest in stocks of troubled companies, new companies and options. High risk.
Growth Funds	Seek capital gains. Invest in stocks of established companies.
Growth & Income Funds	Invest in common stocks of established companies that pay dividends and provide long-term capital gains.
Income Equity Funds	Invest in stocks of companies that consistently pay dividends.
Option Income Funds	Seek high returns from investing in stocks which pay dividends and have call options traded on them.
International Equity Funds	Invest in stocks of companies outside of the U.S.A.
International Bond Funds	Invest in debt of companies outside of the U.S.A.
Global Equity Funds	Invest in both U.S. and foreign company stocks
Global Bond Funds	Invest in debt of U.S. and foreign companies
Balanced Funds	Seek to conserve investors principal, pay current income and seek long-term growth. Invest in bonds, preferred and common stock.
Corporate Bond Funds	Seek high levels of income. Invest in corporate bonds, Treasury and agency bonds.
High-Yield Bond Funds	Seek higher yield by investing in less than investment grade bonds (junk bonds). High risk.
U.S. Government Income Funds	Invests in U.S. Treasury bonds, notes, mortgage-backed securities and other government issues.
GNMA Funds	Invest in government backed mortgage securities.

(Table continues)

How to Invest   175

Table A.1   Continued

FUND	OBJECTIVE
Municipal Bond Funds	Invest in funds issued by state and local governments. Most of the income earned is not taxed at the federal level. There are various maturities of these funds: short-term, intermediate-term and long-term.
Money Market Funds	Invest in short-term instruments sold in the money market such as Treasury bills, CDs and commercial paper. Relatively safe with comparatively high yields.
Index Funds	Seek to match the performance of market indices.
Precious Metal Funds	Invest in stocks of gold, platinum and other mining companies.
Sector Funds	Invest in securities of a specific industry such as technology, health care, defense, etc.

Money Market Funds invest in low risk, short-term debt securities. Debt securities include U.S. Treasury bills, certificates of deposit, commercial paper and banker's acceptances. Due to their short maturities, there is very little fluctuation in the market value of these investments, so money market funds are able to keep the net asset value fixed at $1 per share. Interest earned on these investments less expenses is passed through to shareholders. Money market funds offer a high degree of liquidity (you can withdraw your money at little or no cost), relative safety of your money and a higher rate of return than on savings accounts and bank money market funds.

There are also tax-exempt money market funds which invest in short-term municipal securities and government money market funds which invest in U.S. government securities.

Common Stock Funds invest primarily in common stocks and securities that can be converted into common stocks. Investment objectives vary considerably in common stock funds. At the one extreme are the conservative funds which concentrate on current income and limited capital growth. Then there are the funds that take a middle ground position of investing in stocks which give the fund equal income and

176   Appendix

long-term capital growth. At the other extreme are the aggressive funds which seek long-term capital growth with dividends being of secondary importance.

The net asset value of stock funds will fluctuate on a daily basis due to the volatility of the stock market. A measure of the volatility of common stocks is indicated by their beta coefficients. A beta of one indicates that the stock will do as well or as poorly as the market as a whole. This can be applied to common stock mutual funds. A mutual fund with a beta of 1.25, for example, indicates that the fund is more volatile than the market. Similarly, a fund with a beta of .33 suggests that the fund is 1/3 as volatile as the market. Therefore, you would choose the type of common stock fund depending on your overall capacity to tolerate risk. An investor who can tolerate high levels of risk might go for aggressive funds or sector funds.

Bond Mutual Funds invest in debt securities that provide a fixed return. Bond funds invest in specific types of debt such as corporate debt, Treasury securities, mortgage backed securities, convertible securities, zero-coupon securities, or municipal securities. The maturities of these funds can also vary — short-term, medium-term and long-term, as well as the quality of their investments. There are high risk, high return funds which specialize in low quality debt (junk bonds) and on the other extreme low risk, lower return funds which invest in high quality (investment grade) bonds and notes.

Net asset values of bond funds will fluctuate on a daily basis due to changes in market rates of interest which will cause the prices of bonds and notes to go up or down. Generally, the shorter the maturity, the less the fluctuation in price.

The choice of bond funds will depend on your level of acceptable risk. Longer maturity bond funds face greater risks particularly if market rates of interest fluctuate considerably causing bond prices to fluctuate.

Other Funds There are the hybrid or "balanced" funds which invest in both stocks and bonds. There are also asset allocation funds which move their funds from different types of assets to take advantage of market conditions.

When investing in mutual funds, you can earn a return in three ways:

- through dividends and interest earned by the investments in the fund;

- through capital gains (or capital losses which will decrease the return) when securities are sold by the fund. These gains or losses are generally passed through to the shareholders at the end of the fund's fiscal or calendar year; and

- through the daily fluctuation of the net asset value prices of the shares of the fund where you can sell your shares at a higher (or lower) price than the price that they were bought at.

HOW TO BUY

Mutual funds are sold directly by the investment companies to the public or indirectly through a sales force, brokers, financial planners and insurance agents. Generally, funds which sell directly to the public are *no-load* mutual funds, involving no sales commissions. Almost all money market mutual funds are also no-load. "Load" funds are sold through brokers, and salespeople who charge a commission every time new shares are bought. Brokers, salespeople and financial planners may try to convince you to buy "load" funds because of claims of better performance than no-load funds. There is no evidence to support this premise. If you know which type of fund you want to buy, you should buy a no-load fund and save the commission.

Some funds also charge a redemption fee which is a back-end fee or reverse load for selling shares. If the percentage fees are the same, it may be preferable to go for a reverse load rather than a front-end load because all the money is invested immediately with the former (back-end load).

In addition to management and operating fees, there is another fee which some mutual funds charge called a 12b-1 fee. This is a charge to the fund for marketing and advertising expenses. All of these fees eat into your total return.

A good source of information on mutual funds is a reference book by Wiesenberger called *Investment Companies,* available in most libraries. You can review the long run performance of the funds that you are interested in. Business magazines such as *Business Week, Forbes*, and *Money* publish annual surveys of the performance of the different mutual funds.

If you want to compare the performance of the different mutual funds, you should contact the investment companies (they all have toll free numbers) to request a prospectus for each fund. After studying the objectives of the various funds, compare their performance records and their fees — sales charge and redemption fees, if any, management, advisory, and 12b-1 fees. These fees vary considerably and a fund with a

178   Appendix

higher percentage of fees will have to earn more to compensate for the charges.

ADVANTAGES

- Mutual funds offer investors with small amounts of money diversified portfolios which reduce the overall risks. For instance, investing $2,500 in a common stock mutual fund gives you a share of an excellent cross section of common stocks. You would need to invest at least $50,000 in individual common stocks to have a diversified portfolio.

- Mutual funds provide administrative and custodial duties: record keeping of all transactions, monthly statements, information for tax purposes, as well as the safekeeping of all securities.

- Investment companies always redeem shares at net asset values.

- Portfolios are professionally managed. Many investors may not have the time or the expertise to manage their individual investments.

- There is the advantage of automatically being able to reinvest dividends and interest in the funds or to have them paid out monthly.

- Investors in a family of funds can switch from one fund to another as market conditions change. For example, when interest rates come down, you can switch from your money market funds to common stock funds.

- Levels of risk, return and stability of income and principal vary with the type of fund chosen. However, money market funds offer high liquidity, relative safety of principal and comparatively high money market rates of return.

DISADVANTAGES

- Professional management does not guarantee superior performance. Studies have shown that mutual funds seldom outperform the market over long periods of time and some funds may significantly underperform the market.

How to Invest   179

- When fees and load charges are included, total returns may be significantly less than if you were to purchase individual securities.

- You have no choice over the investment securities that portfolio managers make.

- You have no control over the distribution of hidden capital gains which can upset very careful tax planning. Since investment companies do not pay taxes, income and capital gains (and losses) are passed through to the shareholders.

CAVEATS

- Choose an investment company which has a wide range of funds allowing you to transfer from one fund to another.

- Avoid funds which have sales charges, redemption fees and high management and expense ratios.

CONCLUSION

Investing in mutual funds is good if you do not have enough money to diversify your investments and do not have the time or inclination to select and manage individual securities. In addition to the wide range of funds offered, you can park your surplus cash in money market funds which offer liquidity, relative safety and high money market yields.

7   PREFERRED STOCK

DEFINITION

Preferred stock is a hybrid security which has some features which resemble both common stocks and bonds. As the name implies, "preferred" stock has a preference over common stock with respect to the earnings of the corporation. However, preferred stock is generally non-voting. Preferred stockholders receive their dividend payments before dividends are paid to common stockholders.

Preferred stock is similar to bonds in that it is a fixed income security which pays dividends at either a stated amount (e.g., $2 per share) or as a percentage of its face value (e.g., 8 percent of its $50 face

180   Appendix

value). However, the dividend is paid only if the corporation's board of directors declares dividends, whereas interest on bonds must be paid by the corporation. A corporation's payments of preferred dividends are not legally binding if they are not declared.

Cumulative Preferred is Stock where the dividends accrue if they have been missed in any year. Often when an issue of preferred stock has dividends in arrears, it suggests that the corporation is experiencing financial difficulties. The shares will often trade at a discount and if the company experiences a financial turnaround, there can be an opportunity for capital appreciation in the stock price.

Other types of preferred stock include:

Convertible Preferred is a stock which is convertible into the common stock of that corporation (see the section on convertible securities).

Participating Preferred is stock where preferred stockholders share in the additional profits of the corporation through extra dividends (after the regular dividends have been paid).

Floating Rate Preferred is stock where the dividend rate is tied to an index (e.g., the three-month Treasury bill rate) and dividends will fluctuate up or down.

Noncumulative Preferred stock is a type of preferred stock which is best avoided because if dividends are not paid, they do not accumulate.

Generally, the cost of servicing preferred stock is greater than debt for corporations because the dividends on preferred stock are not a tax deductible expense, whereas interest payments on bonds are tax deductible. Utility companies tend to be large issuers of preferred stock.

If preferred stock does not have a call feature, it may never be retired by the issuing corporation unless the corporation buys the preferred shares back from shareholders on the open market. The call feature allows issuing corporations to buy back their stock at a specified price which usually includes a year's dividends as a penalty.

Some preferred stocks of utility companies have sinking funds to accumulate money for the retirement of part or all of their preferred stock.

HOW TO BUY

Preferred stock, like common stock, can be bought and sold through full service brokerage firms, discount brokerage firms and banks that have brokerage services.

Corporations tend to dominate the market for buying and selling preferred stock due to the 70 percent dividend exclusion for corporations. When corporations buy common and preferred stock of domestic corporations, 70 percent of the dividends received can be excluded from corporate federal taxes. Thus, the market for preferred stock is not as active as the market for common stocks and small lots of preferred stock may be difficult to transact. Preferred stock is not as liquid as common stock or some bonds. Preferred stock is traded on the New York Stock Exchange, American Stock Exchange and the over-the-counter markets.

Commissions charged by brokers are higher for odd lots and less actively traded issues.

Investors can get information to evaluate preferred stock issues from Standard & Poor's, Moody's Investor Services and Value Line, as well as from their brokers.

You can invest indirectly in preferred stock by purchasing shares in mutual funds that invest in preferred stock. Mutual funds offer the advantages of diversification as well as professional management of the portfolio of preferred stock issues.

ADVANTAGES

- Preferred stock generally pays higher dividends than common stock and dividends are relatively assured providing a fixed flow of funds. Bear in mind that preferred dividends are not legal obligations of corporations but they must be paid before any common stock dividends are paid. If the issue is cumulative, dividends in arrears must be paid before common dividends can be paid.

- There is also the possibility of capital gains from investing in preferred stock, especially with the stocks of companies that have omitted their dividends. If such companies improve their earnings, they will resume paying dividends which will result in the appreciation of stock prices.

182   Appendix

- Preferred stock prices are generally less volatile than common stock prices.

DISADVANTAGES

- Preferred stock tends to be less marketable than common stock. This is particularly true for small blocks of shares and thinly traded preferred stocks which can result in higher commissions and spreads for buying and selling.

- Being a fixed income security, preferred stock is subject to interest rate risk — when market rates of interest rise above the preferred stock yield, the price of the stock will fall.

- Since preferred stock is a fixed income security, it does not offer any protection against rising rates of inflation.

- Preferred stock is riskier than bonds since interest payments on bonds are a legal obligation, while dividends on preferred stock are not mandatory obligations of corporations. Furthermore, in the event of corporate bankruptcy, bondholders will have their claims settled before preferred stockholders.

- Yields on preferred stock may be insufficient to compensate for the risks (inflation risk, interest rate risk and risk of default).

- If the company's earnings increase, preferred stockholders do not share in these increases (unless they are participating preferred issues).

- If the issue has a call provision, the company can redeem the stock.

CAVEATS

- In view of the risks, select preferred stock issues of quality companies (at least a BBB rating by Standard & Poor's).

- Always check the features of the call provision of the issue before buying. You could end up paying a higher price for the preferred issue than the redemption amount if it gets called.

CONCLUSION

Preferred stock provides a fixed, steady stream of income. A good time to purchase preferred stock is when it yields a higher rate of return than the same company's common stock.

Due to the 70-percent dividend exclusion received by corporations, it is an advantageous investment for corporations. There are no tax breaks for individual investors.

8 TREASURY BILLS

DEFINITION

Treasury bills (T-bills) are short-term, safe haven investments, issued by the U.S. Treasury and fully backed by the U.S. government. The risk of default is extremely low. In fact, if the U.S. government defaulted on any of its obligations, all investments in the U.S. would be suspect.

Treasury bills are negotiable, noninterest-bearing securities which mature in three months, six months or one year. They are available in minimum denominations of $10,000, and after that in multiples of $5,000.

T-bills are issued at a discount from their face value. The amount of the discount depends on the prices bid in the Treasury bill auctions. At maturity, bills are redeemed at full face value. The difference between discount value and face value is treated as interest income.

The yield on Treasury bills can be determined as follows:

$$\text{Yield} = \frac{\text{Face value} - \text{Price Paid}}{\text{Price Paid}} \times \frac{365}{\text{days to maturity}}$$

A six month Treasury bill purchased for $9,600 and redeemed at face value has an annual yield of 8.33 percent:

$$\text{Yield} = \frac{\$10,000 - 9,600}{9,600} \times \frac{365}{182.5}$$

$$= 8.33 \text{ percent}$$

However, to make matters more complex, bids submitted to Federal Reserve Banks are not quoted on an annual basis, as above, but on a bank discount basis computed as follows:

184   Appendix

$$\text{Yield} = \frac{\text{Face value} - \text{Price Paid}}{100^*} \times \frac{360^{**}}{\text{days to maturity}}$$

* yield is quoted for each \$100 of face value.
** note the use of 360 days as opposed to 365.

Using the same example as above, the discount is \$4 for the T-bill selling at \$96 per \$100 face value with a maturity of six months. The bank discount yield is:

$$= \frac{100 - 96}{100} \times \frac{360}{180}$$

$$= 8.\text{percent}$$

Thus, the bank discount yield is always less than the annual yield.

HOW TO BUY

New issues of Treasury bills can be bought directly from any of the Federal Reserve Banks or indirectly through banks and brokerage firms.

Direct Purchase New issues of Treasury bills are auctioned on a weekly basis by the Federal Reserve Bank and you can submit your bids either on a competitive or non-competitive basis (accepting the average bid at the auction).

Using competitive bids, you will have to submit your bids on a bank discount basis. For example, if you wanted to buy \$100,000 in six-month Treasury bills and pay \$96,000, the competitive bid submitted to the Federal Reserve Bank would be 8%.

The Federal Reserve will then accept those bids which have the lowest discount rates (the highest prices) from all the bids received. Thus, for the accepted bids there is a range of yields, from the lowest to the highest, known as the *stopout yield*,which the Federal Reserve will pay. Investors who have their bids accepted at the "stopout yield" or close to it, will receive greater returns than those received for bids at the lowest yields.

Yields that you bid depend upon the money market rates that are currently being offered by competing short-term instruments as well as expectations of what current short-term rates will be for T-bills. By studying these rates, you have a better chance of submitting a bid that will be accepted. However, with a competitive bid, you face the risk of not having your bids accepted if they are above the "stopout yield."

Less expert investors who may not want to work out their bids or those who want to be assured of purchasing T-bills can submit non-competitive bids. With non-competitive bids, investors are able to buy T-bills at the average accepted competitive bid in the auction. Generally, all non-competitive bids of up to $1 million per investor per auction are accepted, which means that investors are assured of their purchases.

The booklet *Buying Treasury Securities at the Federal Reserve Banks* can be obtained at no charge from the Federal Reserve Bank in Richmond, Virginia. Tender forms to submit bids can be obtained from any of the Federal Reserve Banks and may be sent in mail or in person to the Federal Reserve Banks and branches before the close of the auction.

Upon acceptance of your bid, you'll receive a confirmation receipt from the Federal Reserve. You can then stipulate on the tender form whether you want the Federal Reserve to hold the T-bills in safekeeping or to deliver them. The advantages of buying T-bills directly from the Federal Reserve and holding them to maturity is that you avoid paying commissions or fees.

Buying T-bills at Banks and Brokers T-bills can be bought and sold through banks and brokerage firms who charge fees for their services ranging from $20 to $60 per T-bill. Smaller banks who are not dealers in government securities generally charge higher fees (these banks will have to purchase T-bills from correspondent banks who are dealers). Similarly, small brokerage firms that are not dealers in T-bills charge higher commissions (to cover purchases of these securities from dealers).

Dealers make a market (known as the secondary market) in these securities by buying at the bid price and selling at the ask (higher) price.

The payment of fees or commissions will have the effect of reducing your yields due to the increased amount that you have to pay for the buying or selling of T-bills.

ADVANTAGES

- T-bills provide you with a flexible range of maturities due to the secondary market and complete safety for the repayment of principal and interest.

- T-bills offer excellent liquidity (probably the most liquid of all short-term money market instruments).

186   Appendix

- Interest income on T-bills is exempt from state and local taxation.

DISADVANTAGES

- Although Treasury bill yields are benchmarks upon which the yields of other instruments are based, yields on T-bills tend to be less than those on certificates of deposit for similar maturities and money market mutual funds.

- Treasury bills are subject to interest rate risk. If market rates of interest go up, the price of existing Treasury bills will go down, which may result in capital losses for Treasury bill owners forced to sell before maturity. (If market rates of interest go down, investors who sell before maturity may realize capital gains).

- T-bills do not protect against moderate to high inflation.

CAVEATS

When buying T-bills through banks and/or brokers, shop around for the lowest fees/commissions.

When submitting competitive bids, there is always the possibility that a bid will not be accepted due to unanticipated fluctuations of money market interest rates on the day of the auction.

Although submitting a non-competitive bid assures you of purchase, there is still the uncertainty that you could receive yields well below current yields due to an unexpected drop in short-term interest rates.

CONCLUSION

Treasury bills are safe, liquid short-term investments. (See money market mutual funds, and certificates of deposit for alternative short-term investments.)

9   U.S. SAVINGS BONDS

DEFINITION

Savings bonds are issued and backed in full by the U.S. government. In the 1960s and 1970s when inflation was high, investing in U.S. savings bonds was a patriotic decision rather than a good investment. Rates of return on savings bonds were low and did not equal the returns of other comparable investments. Thus, in order to compete with other investments, the U. S. Treasury increased the rates of interest on U.S. savings bonds.

In 1980, the Treasury issued *EE* and *HH* savings bonds. *EE series* bonds are issued at a discount: a $50 EE bond cost $25 while a $200 EE bond costs $100. Interest is paid at maturity or when the bond is cashed in. The new interest rate (after November 1982) is 85 percent of the average rate paid on five-year Treasury securities. The rate changes every six months but the government guarantees that the rate will not fall below 6 percent if the bonds are held for five years or longer. This provides a floor on the interest rate and if interest rates go up, investors will be able to receive the higher rates. However, if investors do not hold their bonds for five years, they will receive a lower interest rate than 6 percent. Interest is credited every six months (twice a year).

Interest earned on EE bonds can be deferred from federal income taxes until the bonds mature or are redeemed. Interest is exempt from state and local taxes. EE bonds can be used for tax planning purposes and have the following tax advantages:

- By deferring the interest income annually until the bonds are cashed in, you can lower your federal taxable income in the years that you hold the bonds. You can also postpone the tax on the interest income for a further period by swapping the EE bonds at maturity for HH bonds. However, interest received semi-annually on HH bonds is taxable at the federal level each year.

- EE bonds can be purchased for children under fourteen years of age to avoid your children's income being taxed at your marginal tax rates. Children under fourteen years of age pay no tax on investment income under $500. Investment income between $500 and $1,000 is taxed at the lowest rate and amounts over $1,000 are taxed at the parents' marginal tax rates. After fourteen years of age, investment income is taxed at the child's marginal rate. By deferring the interest income until your child turns fourteen years of age, your child's tax liability can be lowered. However, changes are always being being made to the Tax Code so it is important to check with your accountant to determine if this treatment is still in effect.

HH series bonds are only available through an exchange of E, H and EE series savings bonds. (E and H series savings bonds have been

188   Appendix

replaced by EE and HH respectively). HH bonds differ from EE bonds in the following ways:

- HH are issued at par (face) value in larger denominations.

- Interest is received every six months and is subject to federal tax each year.

- Holders receive only the face value at maturity since interest is paid out every six months.

HOW TO BUY

EE savings bonds can be bought (and redeemed) directly through the Bureau of Public Debt or at banks, savings and loan associations and even through employers as payroll deductions. Large denomination bonds are handled through any of the Federal Reserve Banks. The denominations of EE bonds range from $50 to $10,000. The maximum investment in EE bonds is $30,000 per person per year.

HH bonds can be acquired through an exchange of E, H or EE bonds through the Bureau of Public Debt or any of the Federal Reserve Banks or branches. The denominations for HH bonds range from $500 to $10,000.

There are no fees, handling charges or commissions when you buy or sell U.S. savings bonds.

ADVANTAGES

- U.S savings bonds are safe investments; interest and principal are guaranteed by the U.S. government.

- There are no fees, handling charges or commissions to buy and sell.

- Interest earned on U.S. savings bonds is exempt from state and local taxes.

- Interest earned on EE bonds is deferred from federal income taxes until the bonds are redeemed.

- U.S. savings bonds are not subject to interest rate risk.

- You are assured a minimum rate of return of 6 percent on EE bonds held for five years, even if market rates of interest fall below 6 percent and if interest rates go up, you can share in the higher yields.

DISADVANTAGES

- Savings bonds must be held for five years in order to get the floating interest rate. If held for less than five years, you receive the lower rates of interest.

- Savings bonds do not protect against rising rates of inflation.

- The Treasury does not allow savings bonds to be used as collateral and they cannot be transferred as gifts. They may, however, be transferred through an estate.

- Other securities pay higher rates of interest: EE bonds pay 85 percent of the average five year Treasury securities.

CAVEATS

- Compare the returns of other "safe" investments such as Treasury bills and Treasury notes where you may be able to increase your rate of return.

- Since interest on EE bonds is credited semi-annually, you should redeem your bonds after the six-month interest has been paid or credited. If bonds are redeemed before the semi-annual interest is credited, you will lose interest for those months.

- Interest is always credited from the first day of the month, so U.S. savings bonds should be bought at the end of the month to increase the overall rate of return.

CONCLUSION

Savings bonds provide a safe easy way to save money. EE bonds would appeal to you if you are a conservative investor who would like to build up capital and defer current income. HH bonds will appeal to you if you prefer safe investments which pay current income.

REFERENCES

Angrist, Stanley W., and John R. Dorfman. "Investors Tying Strategy to Result of Super Bowl May be Shut Out." *Wall Street Journal*, (December, 1990): 14.

Block, Stanley B., John W. Peavy III, and John H. Thornton. *Personal Financial Management*. Harper & Row, 1988.

Donnelly, Barbara. "Zero Coupon Bonds: Simple Appeal But Not Zero Risk." *Wall Street Journal* (June, 1989).

Francis, Jack Clark. *Management of Investments*. 2d ed., McGraw-Hill, Inc., 1983.

Gottschalk, Earl C. Jr., and Barbara Donnelly. "Despite Market Swings, Stocks Make Sense." *Wall Street Journal* (October, 1989).

Ibbotson, Roger G. & Associates. "Stocks, Bonds, Bills and Inflation" *Yearbook,* Chicago, Ill.: Ibbotson Associates, 1985.

Ibbotson, Roger G., and Gary Brinson. *Investment Markets; Gaining the Performance Advantage*. New York: McGraw-Hill, 1987.

"If Personal Bankruptcy Is Your Only Out." *Business Week*, (January, 1991): 90-91.

Lang, Larry R. *Strategy for Personal Finance*, 4th ed., McGraw-Hill, 1977.

"Looking for a Home Equity Loan? Look Carefully." *Business Week* (April, 1990): 128.

Peers, Alexandra. "How To Take a Junk Bond Plunge." *Wall Street Journal* (November, 1988).

Rowland, Mary. "Speculating in Zero Coupon Bonds.*" New York Times* (July, 1989).

Siconolfi Michael. "Investors Yank Billions from Junk Funds." *Wall Street Journal* (October, 1989).

Slater, Karen. "What Kind of Return can Investors Expect?" *Wall Street Journal* (February, 1989).

_____. "Rating Risk." *Wall Street Journal*, Personal Finance Section (October 20, 1989a).

Slater, Karen and Tom Herman. "Some Muni Holders Trade Up for Safety," *Wall Street Journal* (December, 1990).

"When You Dont Get Credit When Credit Is Due." *Business Week* (October, 1989): 116-117.

Winkler, Matthew. "Junk Bonds Are Taking Their Lumps," *Wall Street Journal* (April, 1989a).

_____. "Campeau Units Junk Shows How Bruised Investors Are Getting Picky." *Wall Street Journal* (May 3, 1989 b).

_____. "Junk Bond Turmoil May Be Here To Stay," *Wall Street Journal* (October, 1989c).

ABOUT THE AUTHOR

Esmé Faerber is an assistant professor of business and accounting at Rosemont College where she has taught for the past four years. She has an MBA degree and is a licensed CPA in Pennsylvania.

She has extensive experience in corporate banking and finance, and public accounting.

She is married and has two children.

Exceptional Titles from the Investor's Quick Reference Series

Mutual Funds Explained: The Basics & Beyond,
Robert C. Upton Jr., $12.95

Wall Street Words: The Basics & Beyond,
Richard J. Maturi, $12.95

Financial Statement Analysis: The Basics & Beyond,
Rose Marie L. Bukics, $12.95

Forthcoming Titles . . .

How Wall Street Works: The Basics & Beyond,
David L. Scott, $12.95, Available in February 1992

Please use order form on next page

ORDER FORM

Quantity	Title		Price

Payment: MasterCard/Visa/American Express accepted. When ordering by credit card your account will not be billed until the book is shipped. You may also reserve your order by phone or by mailing this order form. When ordering by check or money order, you will be invoiced upon publication. Upon receipt of your payment, the book will be shipped. Please add $3.50 for postage and handling for the first book and $1.00 for each additional copy.

Subtotal	
IL residents add 7% tax	
Shipping and Handling	
Total	

Credit Card # _____

Expiration Date _____

Name _____

Address _____

City, State, Zip _____

Telephone _____

Signature _____

Mail Orders to:

PROBUS PUBLISHING COMPANY
1925 N. Clybourn Avenue
Chicago, IL 60614

or Call:

1-800 PROBUS-1